'In this book, Simo Salonen, the distinguished Finnish psychoanalyst, examines the infant's mind and expands theoretical considerations about an individual's psychic survival. Remarkable case presentations illustrate Salonen's metapsychological considerations. His decades long observations on primary identification, psychic trauma, repetition compulsion, mourning, the vulnerability of psychotic individuals, castration anxiety, solving intrapsychic conflict and structural transformation of an individual mind are very informative for all mental health professionals.'

—**Vamık D. Volkan, M.D.**, Emeritus Professor of Psychiatry, University of Virginia and the author of *Would-Be Wife Killer: A Clinical Study of Primitive Mental Functions, Actualized Unconscious Fantasies, Satellite States, and Developmental Steps*

'Dedicated to his severely distraught patients – they suffered from long-term psychosis, psychosomatic conditions, or severe depression – as well as to Freudian metapsychology, Simo Salonen has compiled a breath-taking review of his work as psychoanalyst and psychiatrist during the last 50 years. In success and failure, he helped his patients re-ignite a life-preserving and vitalising 'primal representative matrix.' His book is a unique treatise on Freud's hypothesis of a primary identification, the earliest unconscious impact on the infant of mother or father, or of mother and father. Salonen's book is a labour of love. It is recommended reading for any psychoanalyst or psychoanalytically interested other persons.'

—**David Titelman, Ph.D.**, National Center for Suicide Research and Prevention Karolinska Institutet, Stockholm

Metapsychological Perspectives on Psychic Survival

Metapsychological Perspectives on Psychic Survival explores the integration of traumatic helplessness in the course of psychoanalytic treatment. Based on the author's many years of experience of working with psychotic and severely traumatised patients, this book offers guidelines to approach extreme psychic trauma in the therapeutic setting.

Simo Salonen links psychic representation of the elementary drive phenomena and metaphorical thinking to *primary identification* understood as a mode of object finding. The collapse of this connection signifies a radical psychic trauma, for which integration into the temporal continuity of an individual's life is an essential task for psychoanalysis. Another key element of this book is Salonen's notion of the *primal representative matrix*, referring to a resource of primary narcissism that an individual has been endowed with, carrying vital meanings. Also explored is the crucial *work of mourning*, as the result of which the impoverished ego may recover its primary narcissistic resources.

Using insights from numerous case studies, Salonen offers a new way of understanding severe trauma, which can be used to advance both psychoanalytic theory and clinical practice. *Metapsychological Perspectives on Psychic Survival* will be of great interest to psychoanalysts and psychoanalytic psychotherapists.

Simo Salonen, MD, PhD is a Training and Supervising Analyst of the Finnish Psychoanalytical Society and Adjunct Professor of Psychiatry Emeritus at the University of Turku, Finland.

THE NEW LIBRARY OF PSYCHOANALYSIS
General Editor: Alessandra Lemma

The New Library of Psychoanalysis was launched in 1987 in association with the Institute of Psychoanalysis, London. It took over from the International Psychoanalytical Library which published many of the early translations of the works of Freud and the writings of most of the leading British and Continental psychoanalysts.

The purpose of the New Library of Psychoanalysis is to facilitate a greater and more widespread appreciation of psychoanalysis and to provide a forum for increasing mutual understanding between psychoanalysts and those working in other disciplines such as the social sciences, medicine, philosophy, history, linguistics, literature, and the arts. It aims to represent different trends both in British psychoanalysis and in psychoanalysis generally. The New Library of Psychoanalysis is well placed to make available to the English-speaking world psychoanalytic writings from other European countries and to increase the interchange of ideas between British and American psychoanalysts. Through the *Teaching Series*, the New Library of Psychoanalysis now also publishes books that provide comprehensive, yet accessible, overviews of selected subject areas aimed at those studying psychoanalysis and related fields such as the social sciences, philosophy, literature, and the arts.

The Institute, together with the British Psychoanalytical Society, runs a low-fee psychoanalytic clinic, organizes lectures and scientific events concerned with psychoanalysis and publishes the *International Journal of Psychoanalysis*. It runs a training course in psychoanalysis which leads to membership of the International Psychoanalytical Association – the body which preserves internationally agreed standards of training, of professional entry, and of professional ethics and practice for psychoanalysis as initiated and developed by Sigmund Freud. Distinguished members of the Institute have included Michael Balint, Wilfred Bion, Ronald Fairbairn, Anna Freud, Ernest Jones, Melanie Klein, John Rickman, and Donald Winnicott.

Previous general editors have included David Tuckett, who played a very active role in the establishment of the New Library. He was followed as general editor by Elizabeth Bott Spillius, who was in turn followed by Susan Budd and then by Dana Birksted-Breen. Current members of the Advisory Board include Giovanna Di Ceglie, Liz Allison, Anne Patterson, Josh Cohen, and Daniel Pick.

Previous members of the Advisory Board include Christopher Bollas, Ronald Britton, Catalina Bronstein, Donald Campbell, Rosemary Davies, Sara Flanders, Stephen Grosz, John Keene, Eglé Laufer, Alessandra Lemma, Juliet Mitchell, Michael Parsons, Rosine Jozef Perelberg, Richard Rusbridger, Mary Target, and David Taylor.

For a full list of all the titles in the New Library of Psychoanalysis main series as well as both the New Library of Psychoanalysis 'Teaching' and 'Beyond the Couch' subseries, please visit the Routledge website.

THE NEW LIBRARY OF PSYCHOANALYSIS

General Editor: Alessandra Lemma

Metapsychological Perspectives on Psychic Survival

Integration of Traumatic Helplessness in Psychoanalysis

Simo Salonen

LONDON AND NEW YORK

First published 2018
by Routledge
2 Park Square, Milton Park, Abingdon, Oxon OX14 4RN

and by Routledge
711 Third Avenue, New York, NY 10017

Routledge is an imprint of the Taylor & Francis Group, an informa business

© 2018 Simo Salonen

The right of Simo Salonen to be identified as author of this work has been asserted by him in accordance with sections 77 and 78 of the Copyright, Designs and Patents Act 1988.

All rights reserved. No part of this book may be reprinted or reproduced or utilised in any form or by any electronic, mechanical, or other means, now known or hereafter invented, including photocopying and recording, or in any information storage or retrieval system, without permission in writing from the publishers.

Trademark notice: Product or corporate names may be trademarks or registered trademarks, and are used only for identification and explanation without intent to infringe.

British Library Cataloguing-in-Publication Data
A catalogue record for this book is available from the British Library

Library of Congress Cataloging-in-Publication Data
A catalog record for this book has been requested

ISBN: 978-0-8153-8408-3 (hbk)
ISBN: 978-0-8153-8409-0 (pbk)
ISBN: 978-1-351-20491-0 (ebk)

Typeset in Bembo
by Apex CoVantage, LLC

 Printed in the United Kingdom by Henry Ling Limited

Contents

Foreword	ix
Preface	xii
Acknowledgements	xiv
1 Outlining a conceptual space: an introduction	1
2 On the metapsychology of schizophrenia	12
3 Facing reality: castration anxiety reconsidered	25
4 The restitution of primary identification in psychoanalysis	35
5 The reconstruction of psychic trauma	48
6 The recovery of affect and structural conflict	62
7 Understanding psychotic disorder	75
8 The vulnerable core: the unconscious wish reconsidered	81
9 On destructive drive phenomena: a study of human aggression	91
10 The body and the sense of reality	108

Contents

11 The absent father in the transference: a case study of primary identification and psychic survival   120

12 On the metapsychology of psychic survival   136

13 Reconciliation with the past   153

    Index   169

Foreword

It might not be immediately apparent, but this is a book of opposites.

We are all familiar with the diversity of traditions in psychoanalysis. We also know that this plethora of competing perspectives and conceptual systems has often been represented as a Tower of Babel. We are also familiar with the various ways of solving this problem, including attempts to look for similarities and differences between conceptual systems. What all these attempts have in common is that the authors have started out with different assumptions and perspectives. This book takes us in the opposite direction.

The opposites you are about to meet manifest themselves in many dimensions. First, we have the implicit perspectives, contained in the author's concepts. You will find not only the metapsychology of drives, but also the terms of object relations, not only the language of trauma but also the voice of conflict. There will be topography, as well as structure; much on the attitude of holding, but also on interpretation; an elaboration of the past, but also an evolving treatise on the future. Second, this book encompasses the extremes of psychopathology, exploring not only schizophrenia but also normative crises and challenges in life. Finally, there is the dimension of style. The language is precise, direct, and lucid. On the other hand, one encounters formulations that by their multi-dimensionality and openness come close to poetry. In brief, Salonen's study is redolent of the work of Wilfred Bion.

The author's thinking is comparable to a prism. He does not approach a subject from different points of view; rather, when the reader enters this book, his or her view is analogous to the fate of monochrome light. In passing through the prism, monochrome light reveals its every colour, allowing the heretofore unseen aspects of reality to unfold: here the diversity of psychic reality appears in all its complexity.

The present book is a journey of evolving thought. The themes form a logical sequence, each chapter elaborating points raised in the previous one. Many ideas recur, albeit with various focal points, and as these ideas turn up in a new context, they provide the reader with new insights. Hence, these recurring ideas gain, *nachträglich*, new meaning and force. Even though each chapter of the book echoes different time periods, the author's voice remains surprisingly the same, akin to singers whom time handles gently, with the voice only deepening.

Metapsychological Perspectives on Psychic Survival: Integration of Traumatic Helplessness in Psychoanalysis starts with a treatise on schizophrenia, an essay already presaging some of the book's central themes, focusing on two aspects: a clinical description and a theoretical model of an individual's structural vulnerability underlying the illness. In effect, Salonen shows that schizophrenic fragmentation reveals a vital drive-instinctual foundation – a 'primal representative matrix' – at the border of the somatic and psychic process, which normally remains unnoticed. This matrix is comparable to a loom in textile weaving. One does not see the loom before the weave falls apart. The loss of integrity at this level not only leads to the collapse of the weaving function, but also of inner translucence, akin to a fragmenting windscreen maintaining its contours but losing its transparency. Thus, the usually self-evident foundation of psychic functioning becomes visible in its breakdown.

Consistent with his aim of not remaining on one level, Salonen moves to the other pole of psychic functioning, making two key points: first, the notion of the primal representative matrix is relevant not only in cases of severe psychopathology but also on the level of intrapsychic conflict and the genital reality. The second point implies precisely this fact: as the integrity of our primal representative matrix is a question of psychic survival, and as the genital level of psychic integration is embedded in this vital fundament, we may understand human vulnerability from broader metapsychological perspectives.

In the first three essays Salonen sets the scene by presenting an outline of his themes. Chapter four introduces what Aristotle in his *Poetics* calls *peripeteia*: a turning point. Peripeteia becomes linked to *anagnorisis*, or insight. Through this turn, the reality shows in a new light. In this book, peripeteia emerges through the introduction of *primary identification*.

Primary identification, which is not usually regarded as a central concept, is used not only by Freud but also by, for example, André Green and Eugenio Gaddini. Salonen, however, makes it his own. For him, like Freud, primary identification precedes object relations proper, referring to a moment when the child, in response to the mother's holding attitude, recognises for the first time the object, creating a representational frame for the Other. The child introjects this configuration as a frame for psychic elaboration. Within this frame, the subject becomes established as a metaphor of the object, while this frame, at the same time, upholds one's integrity. To visualise this last point, Salonen takes up an illuminating example: in Inca culture, the world, to remain existent, presupposes that women continue weaving. To be able to weave, a frame and loom are needed.

From this vantage point, Salonen explores the individual's vulnerability, relating it to radical psychic trauma. Closely related to this is the problem of affect integration. The structural conditions for integrated feeling states are not always present, leading to a disintegration of affect-experience. The extreme helplessness discerned in psychosis is analysed from this point, too.

The concluding section of this book testifies to a seldom seen work of integration, encompassing new realms of knowledge, enabling the reader to sense the personal relevance of the issues at hand. The dimensions of body, ambivalence, death, time, and hope form the themes of the concluding chapters.

As the reader may already note, this is a book about integrity and integration in confronting traumatic helplessness. Integrity is not only the central theme of this book but also a characteristic of the book itself. Its author exhibits a very personal way of thinking, which is also lucid. Salonen writes that the transparency of psychoanalytic thinking represents a counterpoint to disintegrating tendencies based on an individual's traumatic past. His book is an illustration of this thesis.

The reader will often be reminded of issues dealt with in preceding chapters. Nonetheless, the recurring themes will always appear a bit different. Reading Salonen's work is analogous to moving in a spiral. On the one hand, we descend more deeply into the material. On the other hand, we reach a higher position from which to see farther. In brief, we move in opposite directions but ultimately attain greater integrity.

Henrik Enckell MD, PhD
Adjunct Professor
Training and Supervising Psychoanalyst

Preface

My purpose in writing this book was to reconsider my clinical experience within the dimensions of psychoanalytic metapsychology from a wide temporal perspective. I have reached a stage in my psychoanalytic career when it is no longer possible to postpone responding to the challenge that temporal limitation on individual life poses for psychoanalytic thinking, a challenge Freud confronted in his later dualistic drive theory, which included his reflections on radical psychic trauma and the problem of psychic survival.

I will focus on the problem of psychic survival in confronting drive-instinctual dangers without being able to integrate them into the sphere of psychic representation, which is the guardian of the pleasure principle and safeguards the individual against radical psychic trauma. However, in less fortunate cases the capacity for psychic representation may fail, with severe consequences. These cases constitute the clinical foundation of my metapsychological studies extending over three decades and including my evolving theoretical conceptualisation of unconscious psychic reality.

Including previous essays in this book without making substantial changes led me to reflect anew on the case histories involved, a process that also turned out to be a work of mourning. Only subsequently was I able to acknowledge that the individual psychoanalytic processes, together with their victories and defeats, belong to my professional past, which made it possible for me to conceive of them as an integrated part of my lifework, analogous to an integrated memory of a lost primary object which enables the ego to perceive the world anew. In this sense, my book can be seen as an integrated

Preface

memory of my psychoanalytic experience shared and lived through with my patients. I hope this process of integration will also provide an answer to the question of what kind of psychoanalyst I have become and what I represent of my own generation.

The specific quality of hope characterising the psychoanalytic method depends on the fact that traumatic ruptures in the past can be dealt with retroactively in the analytic setting, a setting that represents the principle of psychic representation of elementary drive phenomena. Only after being bound through self- and object-representations to an intrapsychic conflict, and resolving this conflict in the transference, these disruptive psychic elements will be bound to promote an individual's psychic survival. What is also at stake is the integration of the fundamental ambivalence towards being itself, leading, if successful, to an integrated memory of the past, restoring a sense of reality and reinvigorating a vital interest in life.

In the following pages, I intend to approach the human mind as a derivative of primary identification, which is understood as a mode of object finding, creating a metaphorical frame of reference for the psychic representation of elementary drive phenomena as well as for solving intrapsychic conflict in the transference. In this sense, primary identification is the first organiser of the human mind, the final organiser being the completed work of mourning, leading to an integrated memory of the lost primary object, marking an individual's psychic survival.

Acknowledgements

I want to thank Professor Alessandra Lemma whose wise editorial comments greatly helped me find the final composition for my work.

I want to express my gratitude to my teachers and colleagues in the Finnish Psychoanalytical Society as well as my analysands for having offered me a genuine opportunity to delve into unconscious psychic reality within the framework of the psychoanalytic setting, an experience that constitutes the subject matter of my metapsychological studies extending over three decades.

I remember with sincere gratitude the late Professor Veikko Tähkä. In our last discussions, he linked the problem of psychic survival to the memory of a lost object, thus inaugurating the theoretical solutions I arrived at later. I also want to thank Dr Henrik Enckell for supporting all my efforts to achieve conceptual clarity in the realm of radical psychic trauma and the issue of psychic survival, as well as for his kind support in shaping my essays into book form. I want to express my deep gratitude to Dr Jacqueline Amati Mehler for her valuable comments on my manuscript, which helped me understand more clearly the significance of the father as a developmental counterpoint to early maternal fusion from the very beginning.

I want to express my sincere gratitude to Dr Jerry Schuchalter for helping me find a suitable expression in English for my psychoanalytic thinking. Our regular meetings have offered a valuable forum for an interdisciplinary discussion on the affinities between psychoanalysis and the human sciences, thus widening my scope outside the psychoanalytic setting.

Acknowledgements

And finally, I want to thank the *International Journal of Psychoanalysis* for permission to use the publication: S. Salonen, 'The metapsychology of schizophrenia', Copyright© 1979 The Institute of Psychoanalysis by permission of John Wiley & Sons Ltd on behalf of The Institute of Psychoanalysis. I also want to thank the *Scandinavian Review of Psychoanalysis* for permission to use the following publications: S. Salonen, 'Facing reality: castration anxiety reconsidered'; 'The restitution of primary identification in psychoanalysis'; 'Reconstruction of psychic trauma'; 'Recovery of affect and structural conflict'; 'Understanding psychotic disorder'; 'On destructive drive phenomena: a study of human aggression', and 'The absent father in the transference: a case study of primary identification and psychic survival' Copyright© The Psychoanalytic Societies of Denmark, Finland, Norway and Sweden by permission of Taylor & Francis, on behalf of The Psychoanalytic Societies of Denmark, Finland, Norway and Sweden. I also want to thank the *Elsevier International Congress Series* for permission to use the publications S. Salonen, 'The human body and the sense of reality'.

1

OUTLINING A CONCEPTUAL SPACE
An introduction

In his essay *Life and the Dialogue*, René Spitz (1963) made a crucial observation regarding the infant's response to its confusion between a living human being and a lifeless surrogate. According to Spitz, this phenomenon, which appears during the second half of the first year of life, marks the infant's new capability to differentiate between a living and an inanimate object. To elucidate this problem, Spitz referred to the excitement and uncanny feeling one experiences visiting a wax museum, where one of the visitors may comically pose as a wax figure and then unexpectedly turns out to be a living human being. To clarify the concept of the object in psychoanalysis, Spitz connected this state of confusion with a subtle non-verbal dialogue between the infant and its mother, where the infant's inner movements elicit a living response and vice versa. Spitz sees human life in general unfolding as a dialogue of this kind, leading to new stages of psychic integration.

In fortunate circumstances, when all is well with the child's early development, the dialogue may proceed smoothly, originally on the level of bodily responses, and later on the level of preconscious meanings capable of becoming conscious after been linked to words, the infant's mother tongue conveying vital meanings. However, even in an ideal case, a child will become exposed to drive-instinctual dangers threatening his or her psychic coherence from within; in a less fortunate case, this may prove to be fateful. André Green's (1986) essay *The Dead Mother* offers a profound exposition of this failure, taking the mother's depression as its starting point. In this context, Green also considered Sigmund Freud's early childhood, when at two years old his younger brother Julius died, causing his mother to face the greatest conceivable loss. This misfortune was also reflected in Freud's later dualistic drive theory where the fundamental dichotomy between life and death constituted a crucial problem, coupled with the magnitude of labour Freud put into solving it (Caropreso and Simanke, 2008).

On the metapsychological starting points

The first key to my metapsychological thinking is the notion of the *primal representative matrix*. This refers to the resource of primary narcissism that an individual has inherently been endowed with, leaning upon vital bodily functions carrying vital meanings and contributing to the sense of being alive (Salonen, 1979). As these meanings are interwoven with subsequent psychic development, this matrix comes to vitalise and constitute both the experiential world as well as the psychic functioning from within, without itself becoming conscious as such. A radical decathexis of this matrix, on the other hand, may have fateful consequences to an individual's psychic and somatic survival, e.g., in psychotic states and life-threatening psychosomatic conditions. Most clearly this becomes visible in schizophrenic disorders, which are the clinical starting point of my metapsychological studies.

The notion of a *primal representative matrix* offers the possibility of clarifying some conceptual difficulties between different psychoanalytic schools, not least the discussion about Freud's dualistic drive theory. Also, Bion's notion of β-elements becomes more understandable when thinking about the drive-economic collapse of this matrix, resulting in a rudimentary ego being exposed to the dismantled drive phenomena devoid of psychic representation. Through a living dialogue between the infant and its mother, these drive elements receive preconscious meanings, enabling them to become integrated into the foundations of the child's emerging mind, i.e. Bion's α-function.

My second key concept is Freud's notion of *primary identification*, which in *Mourning and Melancholia* (1917) was still treated as an oral-incorporative phenomenon. Five years later, Freud (1923) connected primary identification to object-finding before ordinary object ties, which indicates a major transformation in his theoretical thinking: a structural conceptualization of psychic functioning. The reason I adopt Freud's latter conception as my starting point was the observation that even severely disturbed psychotic patients may momentarily recover after recognising the lost primary object in the transference. This startling phenomenon helped me to understand the pivotal importance of primary identification for the capacity of metaphorical thinking. This capability cannot be derived in the first place from the oral-incorporative sphere of psychic experience. Its origins lie in the psychosensory area: the infant first finding the object and, simultaneously, himself as a metaphor of the latter (Laplanche, 1976; Gaddini, 1992). This metaphorical configuration will then constitute an inner frame of reference for the psychic representation of elementary drive phenomena. Only after inventing his structural model was Freud able to integrate the realm of psychic representations and drive-instinctual processes into a functional whole.

In confronting an unexpected fatality, the course of time and the sense of inner movement feels interrupted. Even the subliminal background noise of psychic processes falls silent. In dealing with the problem of temporality in Freud's thinking, André Green (2008) made an essential remark related to this phenomenon, namely, the *sense of movement* characterising psychic processes. At this point, we can return to Spitz's notion of life proceeding as a dialogue. I have visualised this process as a dynamic movement, progressing like an ascending spiral in space and time, attaining new stages of psychic integration in the course of individual life. In unfortunate cases this dialogue may take a negative turn. The negative therapeutic reaction then manifests itself as a descending spiral movement, resulting in disintegration and escalating destruction.

I am inclined to think that an individual's *urge for psychic survival*, which Eugenio Gaddini (1982) associated with the infant's first self-configuration, represents an affectomotor response to the threat of annihilation, containing a potential for aggression. In fortunate cases, this potential will be bound in terms of drive-instinctual dangers to the psychic organisation, first in the sphere of maternal intimacy and later as an integral part of the Oedipus complex, the solution of which finally results in a new kind of psychic autonomy. If this process fails, we are confronted with unbounded aggression and escalating destruction devoid of psychic representation.

The instinctual drives pursue two paths to attain their aim, the first being a direct discharge as actions outside the sphere of psychic representation, and the second as part of evolving psychic organisation to ensure sexual satisfaction on the genital level of psychic integration. The dilemma between these two options reflects an individual's fundamental ambivalence, the integration of which constitutes a crucial point of my metapsychological studies.

Winnicott's contribution

The transference in psychoanalysis with severely traumatised patients often evokes an anachronistic battlefield with such intensity that the setting itself may run the risk of losing its metaphorical significance. What is at stake is an early psychic trauma that has not been integrated as a part of an individual life history; it continues endlessly, possibly resulting in destructive consequences and a depletion of the analysand's psychic resources.

Donald Winnicott (1971) guides us further in understanding this topic, linking an individual's psychic survival to the *mother's survival of the infant's unbound aggression*, the failure of which may result in destructive consequences for the child's future development. In effect, Winnicott derives destructive drive phenomena in general from this failure, as well as including the analyst's failure to survive the analysand's aggression in the transference:

> The essential feature is the analyst's survival and the intactness of the psychoanalytic technique. Imagine how traumatic can be the actual death of the analyst when this kind of work is in the process, although even the actual death of the analyst is not as bad as the development in the analyst of a change of attitude towards retaliation. These are risks that simply must be taken by the patient. Usually the analyst lives through these phases of movement in the transference, and after each phase there comes reward in terms of love, reinforced by the fact of the backcloth of unconscious destruction.
>
> (p. 92)

Winnicott proceeds:

> It will be seen that, although destruction is the word I am using, this actual destruction belongs to the object's failure to survive. Without this failure, destruction remains potential. The word "destruction" is needed, not because of the baby's impulse to destroy, but because of the object's liability not to survive, which also means to suffer the change in quality, in attitude.
>
> (p. 93)

Although Winnicott was perhaps overlooking the accidental misfortunes inevitable in life (Green, 2010) being nobody's fault, his idea of the mother's survival of the infant's aggression is of great importance for our understanding of the child's capacity to deal with destructive drive phenomena later in life. In fact, the mother's survival ensures a resource of healthy aggression at the infant's future disposal, which otherwise would be discharged freely with destructive consequences.

Winnicott's (1975) second notion of *primary unintegration* offers an additional perspective for our discussion. This state of mind differs from psychic disintegration, which signifies a disruptive development. The stage of primary unintegration is characterised by an incoherent state of mind among the multitude of perceptual elements, akin to a dreaming state. During this phase, the mother is perceived as an incoherent human shape reflecting the infant's variable affective tones and colours, which become polarised according to its vital needs. The mother's care-taking presence holds all this together, representing an 'environmental provision' for the child. The mother's failure leaves the infant's rudimentary ego at the mercy of strange psychic elements, which signifies a desolate cosmic experience. Against this background, we can better understand the foundation of an individual's psychic existence, and its vulnerabilities, both of which constitute the subject matter of my metapsychological interest in radical psychic trauma.

Winnicott's (1975) third notion of *primary maternal preoccupation* focuses on a particular change in the mother's personality during the last weeks of pregnancy and continuing for the first weeks after the infant's birth. Although resembling a pathological withdrawal and sensitivity, the primary maternal preoccupation is a normal behaviour pattern, complementary to the infant's stage of primary unintegration. What is at stake is the mother's devotion to the child's physical and psychical needs evolving in this special atmosphere:

> There comes into existence an ego-relatedness between mother and baby, from which the mother recovers, and out of which the infant may eventually build the idea of a person in the mother. From this angle, the *recognition of the mother as a person* [italics mine] comes in a positive way, normally, and not out of the experience of the mother as the symbol of frustration. The mother's failure to adapt in the earliest phase does not produce anything but an annihilation of the infant's self.

> ... In the language of these considerations, the early building up of the ego is therefore silent. The first ego organisation comes from the experience of threats of annihilation which do not lead to annihilation and from which, repeatedly, there is recovery. Out of such experiences confidence in recovery begins to be something which leads to an ego and to an ego capacity for coping with frustration.
> (pp. 303–304)

Winnicott's discussion of the infant's early recognition of its mother as a person refers to primary identification as a mode of object finding. It signifies the emergence of a metaphorical space, corresponding to Winnicott's *potential space*, shared by the infant and its mother. Inside this space, the infant recognises himself as a child of this particular mother, and the mother recognises herself as the mother of this particular child. In short, primary identification does not signify fusion or sameness but *likeness* in the metaphorical sense. Moreover, it creates an inner frame of reference for the psychic representation of elementary drive phenomena as well as concomitant affect states evolving in the infant's mind.

Jan Abram's (2013, p. 311) recent research on Winnicott's archival notes yields an essential observation regarding primary identification. At the end of his life, Winnicott concluded that the imago of the father as a presence in the mother's mind, i.e., the fact of parental intercourse, constitutes an integrative force. In becoming transmitted and internalised as a whole object, it leads to an ego capacity without which there would not be such a thing as survival of the object, in Winnicott's theory, according to Abrams.

Winnicott's view is consonant with Freud's (1923) concept of primary identification relating object finding before ordinary object ties to the father, also suggesting that both parents may be involved. Moreover, Freud associated the emergence of the ego-ideal with primary identification. With Freud's concept as my starting point and based on Gaddini's (1992) and Green's (1986) contributions, I concluded that the capacity of psychic representation depends on primary identification creating a metaphorical frame for the psychic representation of elementary drive phenomena (Salonen, 1989).

Bion's contribution

Thomas Ogden's *Creative Readings: Essays on Seminal Analytic Works* (2012) has clarified my understanding not only of Winnicott's work but especially of Bion's contribution to psychoanalytic thinking. From these starting points, I am going to summarise my view as follows:

According to Bion (1959, 1962), threatening drive elements evacuated from the sphere of solid psychic functioning continue their dismantled existence in exclusion. Through projective identification, however, there opens an opportunity for their integration through the *mother's reverie*. This notion of Bion's refers to the mother's dream-like thinking which is receptive both to her infant's projections as well as her own preconscious responses at the metaphorical level, this signifying a transformation of the psychic processes from the level of β-elements to the sphere of α-function. Thus, the mother's concern for her infant also includes her preconscious dreaming contributing to her child's future capability to think.

Bion's notion provides a key not only to the emergence of the capability for thinking in general, but especially to the analyst's thinking, transposing the psychoanalytic process from the elementary to the metaphorical level of psychic functioning:

If the infant feels it is dying it can arouse fears that it is dying in the mother. A well-balanced mother can accept these and respond therapeutically: that is to say in a manner that makes the infant feel it is receiving its frightened personality back again, but in a form that it can tolerate – the fears are manageable by the infant personality. If the mother cannot tolerate these projections the infant is reduced to continue projective identification carried out with increasing force and frequency. The increased force seems to denude the projection of its penumbra of meaning. Reintrojection is affected with similar force and frequency. Deducing the patient's feelings from his behaviour in the consulting room and using the deductions to form a model, the infant of my model does not behave in a way that I ordinarily expect of an adult who is thinking. It behaves as if it felt that an internal object has been built up that has the characteristics of a greedy vagina-like "breast" that strips of its goodness all that the infant receives or gives, leaving only degenerate objects. This internal object starves its host of all understanding that is made available. In the analysis, such a patient seems unable to gain from his environment and therefore from his analyst. The consequences for the development of a capacity for thinking are serious; I shall describe only one, namely, precocious development of consciousness.

(1962, p. 308)

In coming from outside the early maternal object of fusion, the conceptual language of psychoanalysis represents a 'father tongue' engendering new insights and conceptualisations. This is not, however, possible to attain without consonance between the analyst's conceptual thinking and the ordinary 'mother tongue' spoken in the analytic setting. The psychoanalyst's *reverie* takes place between these two languages, generating insights and deepening psychoanalytic understanding. Thus, the parents' procreative love life is metaphorically present in the analytic setting as a creative potential contributing to the understanding of the analysand's unconscious psychic processes.

Against this background, metapsychology is much more than an abstraction removed from the everyday psychoanalytic experience. It represents a mode of the analyst's preconscious thinking, contributing to the transformation of unconscious psychic processes to the metaphorical level and, thus, within reach of psychoanalytic understanding in the transference.

From the viewpoint of overall psychic organisation, the evacuated drive elements and bizarre objects reside outside the sphere of psychic representation, divorced from normal psychic functioning, indicating abortive drive-instinctual ideas and broken affect states analogous to stillborn babies. They represent an obliterated psychic development dissociated from integrated psychic functioning by a vertical split, eluding psychic representation and metaphorical thinking. The destructive power to which these fragments of thoughts and affects are subject derives from an early superego introject incorporating an individual's unlimited narcissism and delusional omnipotence. From this position, this alluring and persecuting psychic introject escalates internal destruction by attacking (Bion, 1959) vital affects and metaphorical thinking – in the most unfortunate cases, resulting in an individual succumbing to despair, redolent of the devastation caused by the Theban Sphinx in the Oedipus myth.

Concluding remarks

In limiting individual narcissism as well as offering an intrapsychic solution to drive conflict in the transference, the psychoanalytic setting represents a counterpoint to destructive development, resulting in the consolidation of the psychic organisation. This solution is not, however, possible without the escalating destruction first becoming bound in terms of drive-instinctual dangers of separation, castration, and the loss of love to the psychic structure on the advanced level of psychic organisation. With the allure of the Sphinx thus fading, the ego will be given another chance to enter into a genuine dialogue with the lost primary object in the transference. This achievement also signifies the psychic integration of fundamental ambivalence toward the primary object, and simultaneously the capability of differentiation between living and a lifeless object as a precondition for the work of mourning.

The problem of psychic survival will be situated in this book at the crossroads of two drive economic paths, namely a direct discharge through primal phantasies projected into the external world, and the lifelong task of the psychic representation of elementary drive phenomena, providing an intrapsychic solution to drive-conflict. To follow the latter path signifies a consolidation of the psychic organisation and by the same token the integration of fundamental ambivalence. This integration is not, however, cast in iron, but a vulnerable constellation based on primary identification creating a metaphorical space within which an individual can differentiate his or her life experience in temporal and spatial dimensions. The memories of the past, the full intensity of the present, and anticipation of the future are based on this vulnerable constellation, which is inherently susceptible to psychic trauma; I refer to the ego-ideal.

In this book, I will also analyse the unconscious preconditions for the renewal of psychoanalytic thinking from the viewpoint of primary identification, creating a metaphorical space for psychic representation of elementary drive phenomena. Psychoanalysis itself has a future as long as analysts approach the unconscious psychic reality with a newcomer's sense of wonder, and with the same delicate surprise that one can observe in an infant's gaze when it for the first time discovers a human shape in its parents. At such moments also the old, perhaps already forgotten, psychoanalytic writings may regain their lost significance (Salonen, 2007). In this process, the analysts' thinking plays a crucial role. The issue is the transparency of psychoanalytic thinking representing a counterpoint to the disintegrating tendencies based in an individual's traumatic past.

References

Abram, J. (2013). DWD's notes for the Vienna Congress 1971: A consideration of Winnicott's theory of aggression and an interpretation of the clinical implications. In *Donald Winnicott Today*. Abram, J. (editor).

Chapter 14. New Library of Psychoanalysis and the Institute of Psychoanalysis. London: Routledge.

Bion, W. R. (1959). Attacks on linking. *Int. J. Psychoanal.*, 40: 308–315.

Bion, W. R. (1962). The psycho-analytic study of thinking. *Int. J. Psychoanal.*, 43: 306–310.

Caropreso, F. and Simanke, R. T. (2008). Life and death in Freudian metapsychology: A reappraisal of the second instinctual dualism. *Int. J. Psychoanal.*, 89: 977–992.

Freud, S. (1917). Mourning and melancholia. In *The Standard Edition of the Complete Psychological Works of Sigmund Freud*, Volume XIV. London: Hogarth Press and the Institute of Psychoanalysis, pp. 237–258.

Freud, S. (1923). The ego and the id. In *The Standard Edition of the Complete Psychological Works of Sigmund Freud*, Volume XIX. London: Hogarth Press and the Institute of Psychoanalysis, pp. 1–66

Gaddini, E. (1982). Early defensive fantasies and the psychoanalytical process. *Int. J. Psychoanal.*, 63: 379–388.

Gaddini, E. (1992). *A Psychoanalytic Theory of Infantile Experience*. Limentani, A. (editor). London: Tavistock et Routledge.

Green, A. (1983). The dead mother. In: *On Private Madness*. London: The Hogarth Press and the Institute of Psychoanalysis, 1986, pp. 142–173. Reference to *Narcissisme vie: Narcissisme de mort*. Paris: Minuit, 1983.

Green, A. (1986). *On Private Madness*. London: Hogarth Press and the Institute of Psychoanalysis.

Green, A. (2008). Freud's concept of temporality: Differences with current ideas. *Int. J. Psychoanal.*, 89: 1029–1039.

Green, A. (2010). Sources and vicissitudes of being in D. W. Winnicott's work. *Psychoanal. Q.*, 79: 11–35.

Laplanche, J. (1976). *Life and Death in Psychoanalysis*. Baltimore, MD and London: The Johns Hopkins Univ. Press.

Ogden, T. H. (2012). *Creative Readings: Essays on Seminal Analytic Works*. New Library of Psychoanalysis and the Institute of Psychoanalysis. London: Routledge.

Salonen, S. (1979). On the metapsychology of schizophrenia. *Int. J. Psychoanal.*, 60: 73–81.

Salonen, S. (1989). The restitution of primary identification in psychoanalysis. *Scand. Psychoanal. Rev.*, 12: 102–115.

Salonen S. (2007). *A living frame of reference*. A paper read at the Finnish Psychoanalytical Society, 1 September.

Spitz, R. A. (1972). Das Leben und der Dialog. *Psyche – Z Psychoanal.*, 26: 249–264. Reference to Life and the dialogue. *Counterpoint: In Libidinal Object and Subject*. H. S. Gaskill (editor). New York: International Universities Press, 1963, pp. 154–176.

Winnicott, D.W. (1971). The use of an object and relating through identifications. In *Playing and Reality*. London: Tavistock Publications, pp. 86–94.
Winnicott, D.W. (1975). *Through Paediatrics to Psychoanalysis. Int. Psychoanal. Lib.*, 100: 1–325. London: The Hogarth Press and the Institute of Psychoanalysis, pp. 149–154.

2
ON THE METAPSYCHOLOGY OF SCHIZOPHRENIA[1]

My interest in the problem of psychic survival derives from the late 1960s and 1970s when working at the Psychiatric Department of the University of Turku, under Professor Yrjö Alanen. Our goal was to create a psychotherapeutic hospital unit for psychotic patients (Alanen, 1997; Rubinstein and Alanen, 1972; Salonen, 1979). In that context, I had an opportunity to meet with my patients regularly, mostly three times a week for many years and then in my psychoanalytic practice. This book includes the essence of this experience in the form of case histories as a kind of eyewitness account of extreme psychic trauma observed and lived through in the transference. That explains why the schizophrenic disorder came to constitute a paradigm for my psychoanalytic understanding of radical psychic trauma.

The clinical impetus for this essay was the treatment of a hebephrenic young man who had been my patient for seven years. His presentation was characterised by a diffuse brokenness, also manifesting in his physical appearance, which seemed to indicate a deep regression to the stage of primary narcissism or autoerotic fragmentation. Doubtless, a fragmentation of the self-structures described by Kohut (1971) or a loss of self–object differentiation, according to Jacobson (1965), was also present. However, I feel these theoretical notions do not sufficiently explain my experience with this patient, and thus the case seems to be in need of a closer metapsychological analysis.

A young man struggling for his psychic existence

Eli was first admitted to hospital at the age of nineteen, after leaving school on account of a deep psychotic fragmentation which had manifested itself as a withdrawal from shared human reality and bizarre attempts at making his inner world whole again using mathematical formulae and diagrams. When we first met, he told me that the onset of his illness might have been linked to the fact that his twin sister was pregnant and he had imagined he was the child's father.

During the first year, we met three times a week in a hospital setting. Our work was characterised by diffuse fragmentation, which is difficult to describe. His gaze remained clear only for moments, and then became clouded again, while at the same time his skin and psychomotor expression suggested the presence of a profound drive-energetic emergency.

Towards the end of the first year, a remarkable consolidation was perceptible in Eli's incoherent personality. He could now tell me more about the onset of his illness: in the preceding summer, he had been working in a distant locality without many contacts with other people, and there had fallen in love with a girl, although they had never met face to face. Throughout the following autumn, he tried to find this girl everywhere, until he had a psychotic breakdown. The inner image of the girl was, I think, of vital significance for him. I saw it appear and disappear in the course of the therapeutic process as an indicator of his drive-economic and structural conditions. When Eli spoke of this girl, he also told me about his feelings of embarrassment when his brother-in-law told him of his twin sister's pregnancy. His confusion was not only related to his feelings of rivalry towards his brother-in-law, but also his envy of his sister because she had a child.

This more integrated phase soon came to an end and led to a new breakdown during the first summer holiday when we did not meet. During this time Eli preserved the omnipotent delusion that he was a mathematical genius. As before, an extensive loss of inner vitality and psychic coherence followed, indicating his drive-economic emergency. His complexion was once again characterised by a brokenness, evoking the impression of the loss of inner vitality and clarity of thinking.

During the early part of the second year of his treatment, Eli's emotions towards me became more and more polarised into love and hate. During this stage, he was away from the hospital for a short time but had to return after a few months in a very confused state. This confusion was related to Eli's ambivalence towards his father, which manifested itself when he became aware of his tender feelings towards him. In this phase, Eli also felt that his treatment threatened his manliness.

Our third year was characterised by an archaic religious drama, featuring the hero as a prophet, whose unbridled omnipotence put his doctor's and the nursing staff's empathy to a severe test. Eli dressed in sackcloth, indicating penitence, as a result of beginning to experience me as an oppressor similar to his father. On the other hand, the identification with a prophet provided him with the possibility of talking with the mouth of the Almighty against the mighty of this world, while at the same time dissociating himself from his earthly father and me as his representative in the transference.

Still, Eli's sadistic attacks were easier to control than his masochistic attempts to do harm to himself. He would, for instance, keep his feet in ice-cold water or place tourniquets around his legs. When his archaic religiosity temporarily receded, he established a fragile contact with his genuine longings related to the nursing staff and me. However, these feelings were soon concealed again by guilt and his bizarre preaching about the law and damnation, one aspect of which was to evoke fearful awe among spectators.

Towards the end of the third year, Eli's inner conflict culminated in his driving a nail into his foot as a bizarre gesture of atonement. This act led to a severe infection, and the physical treatment of this infection, together with compresses and baths, apparently marked one of the turning points in his treatment. Eli was now able to accept bodily intimacy without overwhelming anxiety and feel at the same time that his foot was being cared for, which also formed a counterbalance to his castration anxiety. With the healing of his leg, Eli's bizarre religiosity receded, and he began to study the Bible in a more genuine way. By the end of the third year, his personality appeared cheerful and lucid. After being discharged from the hospital he resumed his interrupted studies.

The crisis described above reflected Eli's major efforts to organise his chaotic Oedipal constellation in the therapeutic setting by creating psychic representations for his libidinal longings and finally by binding his castration anxiety to more stable psychic structures. Eli's heroic struggle was apparently related to his masturbation, which evoked not only castration anxiety in him but also the fragility of his bodily self. An important part of the explanation lies in the fact that Eli's early maternal care was defective because of his mother's psychosis.

The first part of the fourth year of our work was a comparatively harmonious period. Eli was now able to recollect the girl he had fallen in love with and relate to how empty he felt after leaving school. On the other hand, he considered that he had found in the Bible the meaning of life, which he had lost when he dropped out of school. Consequently, he began to have his Bible always with him and talk excitedly about what he had read. The Bible plainly signified a transitional object in this phase (Winnicott, 1953).

At first, Eli did well in his studies, which was perhaps one of the reasons why his intrapsychic conflict accentuated. As a result, he relapsed into a fragmented state, which necessitated his readmission to hospital. After the worst period of fragmentation lasting a few weeks had passed, he began to experience me as a superior adversary.

The Bible and Eli continued to belong inseparably together, and now he began to search for glorifying attributes and combine these into poems of praise, which he then read to me with his eyes sparkling. When I began to confront Eli with his idea of me as a superior adversary, he associated this with an appendectomy he had undergone at the age of 10, and it occurred to him that his old desire to become a surgeon was perhaps connected with this operation. Towards the end of the fourth year, he recalled that the onset of his illness several years previously had been related to an incident at school when the teacher showed pictures of towers, which made him want to laugh, as these caused him to think of a penis. Eli's male characteristics were in the foreground during this phase. Despite this phallic consolidation, Eli still had plenty of omnipotent fantasies, and his relationships with other people were predominantly narcissistic. In addition to these qualities a frail sort of object attachment characterised his relationship to me, though this was something that we could not yet talk about directly.

The next three years of Eli's treatment revealed the extensiveness of his structural problems. The failure of his central ego functions and the collapse of his inner *representational world* (Sandler and Rosenblatt, 1962) explain why the relative psychic coherence and inner vitality brought about through much work disappeared from time to time, though no longer without a trace. Instead, it returned richer when his treatment was continued. A process of internalisation was going on, in the course of which Eli was able to internalise his present experience to his representational world, as a result of which the conditions for his psychic functioning gradually improved.

Eli's coherence, albeit frail and brittle, made it increasingly possible to discuss his images of both himself and me as separate individuals. It was also possible to analyse his religious beliefs and conceptions more carefully. The gradual recovery of Eli's inner experience took place alongside the Bible. The Holy Scripture was for him the only authoritative understanding of life, analogous to a parent's interpretation of reality for their child.

Eli's spiritual struggle, of course, played out in the transference in a variety of ways. The Bible indeed represented for him an idealised self-object, as described by Kohut (1971), which as a result of transmuting internalisation came to enrich the various capabilities at his ego's disposal. The defensive character of his spiritual struggle was also significant in maintaining his fragile and brittle object ties. The Bible had, however, an even more elementary psychological significance enabling him to create and maintain psychic representations when the primary object providing care for him was not present. Eli used the 'living word' to enrich and strengthen those elementary structures sustaining his psychic existence, the permanence of which depends on the individual's prior as well as current experience of the other people's world.

Delineation of the clinical material

Initially, I will seek to provide a more concrete and detailed picture of the schizophrenic patient's experience of the loss of inner vitality and the collapse of the experiential world. This catastrophic experience signifies not only inner emptiness but also a feeling of being exposed to a kind of cosmic desolation. Metaphorically speaking, the patient's rudimentary ego is then in touch with the background noise of unconscious psychic processes, which for the imploded and impoverished ego is a highly traumatic experience.

Through the study of traumatic narcosis experiences during surgery, it is possible to gain valuable insight into an analogical non-schizophrenic state. Here I have two patients in mind, the first of whom fell into a strange state where he experienced himself as being in the midst of celestial bodies dashing at tremendous speeds. In the second case, on the other hand, the operating surgeon's last words kept repeating themselves in the patient's ears at an accelerating frequency, until he lost consciousness. The sound itself felt mechanical, with no human tone, and the experience as a whole was extremely traumatic. In both examples, the patients' associations lead to the idea of castration, which is understandable in the case of surgery. It seems probable that in these cases the narcotic state was induced by a decathexis of the primal representative matrix and that the patients only fell asleep after this.

In a schizophrenic disorder, this phenomenon is, of course, more complicated, since the pathological process also mobilises primitive defences to protect the ego in this emergency. Thus, for instance, a regression to early object relations and primitive narcissism may form the ultimate line of defence from which the impoverished ego is still able to take care of its regulatory functions. Likewise, the ego-split may be the only possibility of foreclosing those areas which form a sort of Bermuda triangle, a maritime area where ships disappear without a trace, so that nobody can return to relate the circumstances of their disappearance.

I will now return to consider the change in Eli's physical appearance, which was characterised by his lifeless skin and the peculiar disorganisation of his facial expressions, particularly around the mouth, which gave the impression of diffuse fragmentation and a loss of inner transparency. What repeatedly attracted my attention is that this enigmatic state was worse in the morning. This observation may be theoretically important, as well as the fact that it was imperative for Eli to have an opportunity to read his Bible undisturbed in the morning to recover his inner vitality after a night's sleep.

Focusing the metapsychological approach

My metapsychological framework for understanding this patient is, in the first place, drive-economic, and secondarily, structural and dynamic (Freud, 1915c). I shall devote particular attention to those phenomena that form a basis for inner vitality, the permanence of psychic organisation, and the facility of psychic functioning. My analysis will focus on the earliest representatives of the instinctual drives, which are hardly accessible by verbal communication in the transference. My goal is to map the area beyond the solid psychic structures and constituting the drive-energetic foundation for them. This part of psychic reality is possible to approach in conditions such as schizophrenia where the foundations of psychic functioning have become radically endangered.

In his work *On Narcissism: An Introduction*, Freud (1914) described many unconscious psychic phenomena that have later proved to represent the main avenues of psychoanalytic research. In this paper, he also presented his view of schizophrenia as a radical decathexis of the inner object ties. Using this model, he explored the earliest drive phenomena, approximating the somatic processes, which also forms the subject matter of my present considerations. Moreover, Freud discussed the controversy between the monistic versus dualistic drive theories and raised the possibility of undifferentiated psychic energy.

Edith Jacobson (1965) examined Freud's concept of primary narcissism, forming the hypothesis that the earliest stage of psychic development is likely to be characterised by an *undifferentiated drive-energetic discharge* taking place through physiological channels which are difficult to define in greater detail. Only when the child's development proceeds, does this process begin to cathect the drive elements that will later manifest themselves as unconscious psychic reality. According to Jacobson, the primary drive potential will simultaneously become differentiated into libidinal and aggressive strivings, which then, when they have become fused and neutralised in various ways, exhibit vicissitudes and functions of their own in the overall psychic organisation.

According to Edith Jacobson, a reverse development – a drive-energetic regression – occurs in psychoses, leading, via de-fusions and de-neutralisations, to an undifferentiated state bearing a resemblance to the initial state, in which the discharge of drive energies will again take place on the physiological level. In this connexion, Jacobson referred to Max Schur (1966), who had studied the psychosomatic disorders from the viewpoint of drive-energetic regression. Schur argued that psychosomatic illness and schizophrenia are analogous in the sense that in both cases a regression and a drive-instinctual de-fusion has taken place, which implies a *re-somatisation of affect responses*. Schur further argues, influenced by Hartmann's (1953) views, that the freed aggression is likely to occupy a prominent place in this context. Jacobson solved the problem of the interrelation between libido and aggression at the deepest level of regression by proposing that they cannot be differentiated from each other. My present study has profited from Edith Jacobson's drive-economic formulations, particularly her notion of drive-energetic regression in the psychoses, and the instinctual drive discharging anew through unknown physiological channels.

Next, I will consider the stage of early psychic development from the viewpoint of the rudimentary ego. I think this comes close to what Freud had in mind when in *Instincts and Their Vicissitudes* (1915a) he referred to the 'original reality' ego, which will be replaced by the 'purified pleasure-ego'. I paraphrase Freud's view as follows:

Despite the protection provided by the inborn stimulus barrier and adequate maternal care, the infant is unable to master alone the stimulation arising from within its body, which soon grows unbearable. The infant is defenceless against this stimulation and is still unable to alter external realities. To survive this traumatic situation, the rudimentary ego creates the first mental images or psychic representations of the relief-bringing help, of which it already has experience. The 'original reality ego', thus, begins to form a representational world by cathecting the memory traces of its contact with relief-bringing external reality and the reality of its own body. Thus, a remarkable expansion takes place in the realm of the rudimentary ego. It obtains entirely new kinds of preconditions for its future development towards advanced psychic functioning. Enrichment of the representational world and the establishment of different psychic functions form a necessary prerequisite for this development. The ego will thus obtain tools and means for discharging its function as a mediator vis-à-vis reality. On the other hand, it will be charged with new regulatory tasks that may prove too demanding for it to perform.

In his next metapsychological paper *On Repression* (1915b), Freud dealt more closely with the problem of psychic representation. According to him, the first ideational representative of the instinctual drive exists beyond *primal repression* without ever becoming conscious:

> We have reason to assume that there is a primal repression, a first phase of repression, which consists in the psychical (ideational) representative of the instinct being denied entrance into the conscious. With this a fixation is established; the representative in question persists unaltered from then onwards and the instinct remains attached to it. . . .
>
> The second stage of repression, repression proper, affects mental derivatives of the repressed representative, or such trains of thought as, originating elsewhere, have come into associative connexion with it. On account of this association, these ideas experience the same fate as what was primally repressed. Repression proper, therefore, is an after-pressure. Moreover, it is a mistake to emphasise only the repulsion which operates from the direction of the conscious upon what is to be repressed; quite as important is the attraction exercised by what was primally repressed upon everything with which it can establish a connexion. Probably the trend towards repression would fail in its purpose if these two forces did not

co-operate, if there were not something previously repressed ready to receive what is repelled by the conscious.

(p. 148)

I have understood the previous passage to say that psychic organisation is a derivative of what is primally repressed. Metaphorically speaking, the whole experiential world becomes interwoven with this. This development does not, however, mean that the primally repressed would cease to exist, but, instead, it exerts a permanent influence on all psychic activity, which it also sustains and vitalises. It constitutes a kind of *basic psychic tissue* or *primal representative matrix*, which will be repeated throughout the entire representational world and psychic functioning. I suggest that this amorphous matrix may preserve its connection with the somatic process, transforming it to the psychic level. The sense of being alive derives from this process.

Freud (1926) returned to this topic when considering his structural theory, positing that primal repression and signal anxiety at the ego's disposal are at polar ends of a regulatory system which manages the entire drive economy. This polarity makes it possible for the ego to regulate psychic processes by summoning the pleasure-unpleasure principle to respond to instinctual dangers in a similar way to which it responds to imminent psychic trauma, that is, by reinforcing the countercathexis of primal repression.

Freud discussed the first psychic representative of the instinctual drive and its later derivatives from the viewpoint of anti-cathexis, without in this connection paying attention to the possibility that the primal drive representatives may also lose their cathexis. The attraction which Freud attributed to primal repression could in part be explained by the withdrawal of cathexes and the instinctual drive regressing to approach somatic processes, resulting in a depletion of drive-instinctual resources throughout the psychic organisation.

An attempt at a metapsychological definition

Nathanael London's (1973) essay on the psychoanalytic theory of schizophrenia is helpful in understanding the nature of this disorder. His starting point is the patient's incapacity to organise memory traces into mental representations (specific schizophrenia theory). From the viewpoint of research, it is not fruitful, London argued, to apply the general psychoanalytic view to schizophrenia, which maintains that a psychosis represents the defence of an exceptionally helpless ego when it is confronted with an overwhelming intrapsychic conflict, causing the ego to relinquish its objects in a radical way (unitary schizophrenia theory). Judging by my clinical experience, however, such a theoretical dichotomy may not be necessary. It would rather seem that these viewpoints form a dynamic whole. Only a careful analysis of the economic and structural conditions in the course of the therapeutic process can reveal where the focus of psychotic disorder lies in each case.

Willi Hoffer (1952) has shed further light on our topic. He compared the psychotic decathexis to the newborn infant falling asleep, in which case the emerging representational world disappears without trace, and the infant has to recreate it on waking, until structural development makes maintaining psychic representations possible. In the case of an adult psychotic patient, the persistence of the representational world is in large measure dependent on subsequent structural achievements, too. If our interest is focused exclusively on early pathology, we risk ignoring the later vicissitudes of instinctual drives, which underlie the entire psychic organisation like a vault. It is not without good reason that Edith Jacobson attributes great importance to the consolidation of the superego and the ego-ideal during adolescence, which constitutes, in her opinion, the final safeguard against a total collapse of the psychic organisation. Along with the genital primacy attained during adolescence, optimal drive-economic conditions will finally be assured. Despite the fact that in the schizophrenic patient, this structural achievement remains frail and defective, it still forms a dynamic counterweight to his or her early pathology and contributes to maintaining his psychic coherence (Salonen, 1976).

I will now return to the polarity of psychic regulation and the significance of signal anxiety. This anxiety derives its origin from the unconscious drive-instinctual dangers ultimately subordinated to the fear of castration. An adequate working through of the transference presupposes that these dangers have been bound through self and object representations to the psychic structure. If successful, this structural achievement will supply drive-instinctual resources at the ego's disposal for the performance of its regulatory tasks. In the case of a schizophrenic patient, this process has failed, as a result of which the degree of drive-instinctual neutralisation is low (Hartmann, 1953). The impoverished ego will then be left at the mercy of traumatic stimulation, signifying that the scope of psychic regulation has remained too limited.

A successful analytic reconstruction and a working through of the drive-instinctual dangers of separation, castration, and the loss of love may result in the unfolding of the psychotic structure in the transference. It has been of particular interest to observe that the analysis of castration anxiety during the later stages of treatment may signify a decisive step towards the patient's ego autonomy, suggesting that signal anxiety will no longer disintegrate into its primitive forerunners.

A psychoanalytic exploration of the realm beyond primal repression encounters great difficulties. Anna Freud (1969), for instance, considered success in such an endeavour doubtful. Schizophrenia, however, offers the possibility to approach this frontier of psychoanalytic knowledge indirectly, insofar as the decathexis of this area is involved in this illness, as presented above. It seems probable that the principle of creating living psychic connections has its first representatives within the sphere of the primally repressed. Perhaps these representatives have come into being as a result of accomplishments of the rudimentary ego in attempting to gain control over the imminent psychic trauma. One of the essential characteristics of primal representative matrix would then be the creation of living connections and a striving for synthesis throughout the psychic organisation. Schizophrenic fragmentation, on the other hand, would be intimately connected with the collapse of this function.

To conclude this chapter, the enigma of schizophrenic fragmentation is related to the particular vulnerability of psychic regulation. The instinctual dangers inevitable in individual life may, therefore, precipitate the future schizophrenic to a drive-economic emergency, the starting point of which is the decathexis of the primal representative matrix. As a result, the drive-instinctual process becomes channelled through a short circuit, as it were, approximating the somatic processes and depleting vital psychic resources.

As the entire psychic organisation is, metaphorically speaking, interwoven with the primal representative matrix, the collapse of this matrix has far-reaching consequences throughout the entire representational world. The disorder will manifest itself as a radical disappearance of inner vitality, a breakdown of ideational contents, and a loss of functional capabilities. Schizophrenic fragmentation does not amount, in the first place, to a split on the macro level, but to a diffuse brokenness throughout the psychic organisation. I have compared this phenomenon with the shattering of a windscreen of a car that, after having been fragmented, may keep its contour, but lose its essential functional property, namely, transparency. Just as a fragmented windscreen is discernible to the driver, the primal representative matrix becomes perceptible in schizophrenic fragmentation, and not before.

Note

1 The first version of this paper was read at the Finnish Psychoanalytical Society, December 1976, and published in the *Int. J. Psychoanal.*, 60: 73–81 (1979). Copyright© 1979 The Author, Journal compilation Copyright© 1979 The Institute of Psychoanalysis. Reprinted by permission of John Willey & Sons Ltd on behalf of The Institute of Psychoanalysis.

References

Alanen, Y. O. (1997). *Schizophrenia: Its Origins and Need-Adapted Treatment.* London: Karnack.

Freud, A. (1969). Difficulties in the path of psychoanalysis: A confrontation of past with present viewpoints. In *The Writings of Anna Freud,* Volume 7. New York: Int. Univ. Press, 1971, pp. 124–156.

Freud, S. (1914). On narcissism. In *The Standard Edition of the Complete Psychological Works of Sigmund Freud,* Volume XIV. London: Hogarth Press and the Institute of Psychoanalysis, pp. 67–102.

Freud, S. (1915a). Instincts and their vicissitudes. In *The Standard Edition of the Complete Psychological Works of Sigmund Freud,* Volume XIV. London: Hogarth Press and the Institute of Psychoanalysis, pp. 117–145.

Freud, S. (1915b). Repression. In *The Standard Edition of the Complete Psychological Works of Sigmund Freud,* Volume XIV. London: Hogarth Press and the Institute of Psychoanalysis, pp. 146–158.

Freud, S. (1915c). The unconscious. In *The Standard Edition of the Complete Psychological Works of Sigmund Freud,* Volume XIV. London: Hogarth Press and the Institute of Psychoanalysis, pp. 159–215.

Freud, S. (1926). Inhibitions, symptoms and anxiety. In *The Standard Edition of the Complete Psychological Works of Sigmund Freud,* Volume XX. London: Hogarth Press and the Institute of Psychoanalysis, pp. 75–176.

Hartmann, H. (1953). Contribution to the metapsychology of schizophrenia. *Psychoanal. Study Child,* 8: 177–198.

Hoffer, W. (1952). The mutual influences in the development of ego and id: Earliest stages. *Psychoanal. Study Child,* 7: 31–41.

Jacobson, E. (1965). *The Self and the Object World.* London: Hogarth Press.

Kohut, H. (1971). *The Analysis of the Self.* New York: Int. Univ. Press.

London, N. J. (1973). An essay on psychoanalytic theory: Two theories of schizophrenia. Part I and II. *Int. J. Psychoanal.*, 54: 169–193.

Rubinstein, D. and Alanen, Y. O. (1972). *Psychotherapy of Schizophrenia.* Amsterdam: Excerpta Medica.

Salonen, S. (1976). On the technique of the psychotherapy of schizophrenia. In *Schizophrenia 75.* Jörstad, J. and Ugelstad, E. (editors). Oslo: Universitetsforlag, pp. 115–133.

Salonen, S. (1979). Psychotherapeutic studies in Schizophrenia. *Annales Universitatis Turkuensis*, Ser. D, 12.

Sandler, J. and Rosenblatt, B. (1962). The concept of the representational world. *Psychoanal. Study Child*, 17: 128–145.

Schur, M. (1966). *The Id and the Regulatory Principles of Mental Functioning.* New York: Int. Univ. Press.

Winnicott, D.W. (1953). Transitional objects and transitional phenomena – a study of the first not-me possession. *Int. J. Psychoanal.*, 34: 89–97.

3

FACING REALITY
Castration anxiety reconsidered[1]

In this chapter, I shall examine the child's developing ego in relation to the genital reality and the significance of castration anxiety in this context. The unconscious idea of castration is a ubiquitous threat towards the development of an integrated love life. It is only after integrating this threat into an advanced psychic organisation that the comprehension of genital reality and full participation in it becomes possible. The horror evoked by the threat of castration may be connected with the idea of ultimate exclusion from this participation.

The relationship of the parents as representative of genital reality

The perceptible atmosphere into which the child is born and with which it has rudimentary contact is created by the parents' genital relationship. The child's first perceptions of this relationship are coenesthetic in nature and based on 'id-perception' (Freud, 1940a), through which the child has subliminal contact with its parents' unconscious psychic processes. It is believable that in this early phase, the mother is in the foreground, and it is her unconscious that forms the child's first psychic reality (McDougall, 1978).

Laplanche's (1976) study of the origins of sexuality from the viewpoint of seduction led him to conclude that early maternal care leads not only to the stimulation of the infant's erogenous zones but that particular sexual meanings from the adult world may also intrude into the infant's emerging mind, where retroactively they achieve personal meanings in the course of individual life. According to Laplanche, this provides a key to Melanie Klein's (1928) observations on the early Oedipus complex on the part-object level. Indeed, it is conceivable that the mother's Oedipus complex and its archaic ideational contents are within the grasp of the infant's id-perception. In this way, the child might also receive the first hint of the father's genital importance, according to Laplanche.

On this basis, we can understand why the idea of castration seems to be ubiquitously associated with human sexuality. It is embedded in the matrix of psychic interaction into which we are born and in which our psychic development takes place. I am inclined to think that Freud's (1926) notion of castration as a realistic danger implies that it forms an intrinsic part of unconscious psychic reality. Moreover, Freud (1913, 1938) related the idea of castration to an early phase of human evolution; that is, that period when exogamy became law and incest a terrifying possibility.

Primal scene phantasies reflect the child striving to organise his non-integrated sexual excitement in relation to his parents' love life. This implies not only the child's bodily excitations but also those sexual and aggressive strivings having begun to live a psychic life of their own within him: that is, instinctual drives. It is in this context that the idea of castration receives its affective and ideational meanings, while at the same time forming the final obstacle to realising the Oedipal wishes.

Oedipal renunciation occurs under the threat of castration and humiliation (Freud, 1924). This signifies the most painful loss, a true *Untergang*, which the child has to work through to retain its integrity in relation to genital reality. There is a danger that instead of this renunciation, the child's helpless ego will resort to a destructive solution, comparable to the cutting of the Gordian Knot. Instead of psychic transformation, the libidinal ties to reality become severed with serious structural consequences: exactly what occurs in the case of psychoses and in a more limited way in sexual perversions. Instead of the solution of the Oedipus complex, the Oedipal constellation as a whole becomes abolished. To find a viable solution, the child's ego has to be capable of a transformation consonant with the genital reality represented by the parents.

Joyce McDougall (1980) crystallised the pain of Oedipal surrender as follows:

> In the best of all possible worlds the child will of course eventually accept that what he wishes were true will never be true; that the

secret of sexual desire lies in the mother's missing penis; that only the father's penis will ever complete her genital, and he will for ever be alienated from his primary sexual desire and his unfilled narcissistic wishes.

(p. 74–75)

After being confronted with genital reality, a new clarity also falls on the problem of castration. When losing the infantile belief in phallic monism – that is, that originally all human beings have a penis – the sexual relationship between the parents becomes comprehensible for the child. Janine Chasseguet-Smirgel (1985) characterised this new constellation almost poetically as the 'Father-Creator's genital world', a universe where the parents have a procreative task to fulfil. To illustrate my point, I am going to present two clinical examples.

As a child, a male analysand of mine believed that babies are born from a new orifice opening up in the mother's perineal area, which normally is 'blank', as he put it. While he was talking about this, he felt his anxiety diminishing. I then asked him if his anxiety could be related to a recent genital operation that he had undergone, and which he perhaps had associated with castration. The same connection had also occurred to him, and he proceeded to say he had always thought of his mother's femininity as blank. I paused here and asked if the 'blankness' of his mother's genital area might also mean that his father was not necessary. This theme had been dealt with earlier during his analysis. His immediate response was: 'It's odd that now I can first think about sexual intercourse between them.' The disavowal of his parents' genital love life had been linked with my analysand's high narcissistic vulnerability which became accentuated in the transference because of his minor genital operation.

As a result of comprehending the parent's love life, a new perspective falls into place, expanding the child's inner world and bringing an aspect of joy. Henceforth, the way is opened up for sexual identifications without guilt, both in the masculine and feminine sense. The idea of castration also takes on a new, metaphorical meaning.

The psychoanalytical setting represents metaphorically the genital reality against which the analysand's transference becomes analysed. Moreover, it also represents the Oedipal solution, bringing it within reach of the analysand's comprehension.

My second vignette comes from the final stages of the successful analysis of a female patient in her thirties. After having been involved in a masochistically tinted relationship with her mother, she was finally able to reconstruct in the transference the value her parents' love life had in her own sexual life. Unfortunately, their relationship had broken down when she was five years old. This reconstruction was based on the fantasies and ideas that she had of the relationship between my wife and me, a relationship which was also the source of her intense envy, and of castration anxiety for her. The new clarity she had gained in her analysis enabled her to remember and mourn the short-lived time when her parents' relationship could still be perceived as a source of vital interest.

The frightening aspect of genital love life

Castration anxiety is a touchstone of the ego's integrity. In his description of the ego-split, Freud showed that an avoidance of reality was related to the child perceiving the female genital and the ensuing castration anxiety (1927, 1940b). Appalled by this sight, the child tends to dismiss the shocking experience and cling to a belief in phallic monism by constructing a fetish for this purpose. Then, the ego has 'seeing eyes yet does not see' and 'hearing ears yet does not hear'. Through the fetish, the child persuades himself, and perhaps other people, that the problem of castration need not be taken seriously. Such a solution is of course spurious, since it is motivated from the very onset by the threat of castration. On the other hand, the shattering of the fetishistic construction is a highly traumatic experience revealing the ego's helplessness when faced with genital reality, the significance of which the child has not been able to integrate into his or her understanding. Also, there is a feeling of shame for having constructed the fetish, which one preconsciously knows to be counterfeit.

McDougall emphasised the importance of the fetish and the 'neo-sexualities' related to it in sustaining individual identity when the alternative would be uncontrolled annihilation anxiety and the dissolution of primary identification. Like Freud, McDougall locates the roots of castration anxiety in the infant's primordial loss: the loss of the mother's breast. McDougall showed that this loss also becomes subsumed under the psychic modality of castration in the course of a psychoanalytic treatment (McDougall, 1974, 1980, 1986).

Janine Chasseguet-Smirgel (1974) emphasised the anal-destructive character of the fetish. According to her, the goal of the fetishistic solution is to devalue the parents' procreative love life and to deny the significance of difference between the generations. In her view, the fetish represents the idealised anal phallus, which is ultimately shown to be a sterile and lifeless counterfeit of the living penis, functioning to sustain the omnipotent belief in one's invulnerability. When Chasseguet-Smirgel argues that in the unconscious, anality and death belong inseparably together in the same way as castration and life, she is expressing an idea also central to my theoretical thinking: namely, that the psychic integration of individual vulnerability, and its id-level counterpoint castration, constitute the crux of psychoanalytic endeavour.

The dismantling of the fetishistic solution in psychoanalysis is comparable to the child's original castration shock, as the ego is confronted with genital reality and is no longer able to find assurance in the ego-split and self-deception. How the analysand copes with this confrontation depends crucially on the extent to which he or she has succeeded in establishing a separate psychic existence. The more fragile this developmental achievement, the more the castration shock tends to escalate into psychic trauma. On the other hand, with an increase in ego strength, the threat of castration is aimed at the Oedipal desire, where individual vulnerability is felt most acutely.

Castration occupies a specific position among the instinctual dangers because it will in the last resort subordinate other instinctual dangers. For this reason, even psychotic pathology becomes ultimately integrated into this context. The same applies, according to Freud, to the individual's mortality, which becomes linked in the unconscious with the idea of castration. Thus, castration anxiety forms the narrow gateway not only to genital integrity but also to understanding human vulnerability in general.

The dissociation of the idea of castration leads to distortions in experiencing one's body, in particular, the genitals. The psychic integration of this idea, on the other hand, restores living contact with the body and its functioning, while sexuality takes on not only the quality of playful pleasure but also all the seriousness belonging to it. This seriousness means the awareness of possessing and using of the capabilities not only for acts of love, but also for acts of destructiveness: abandonment, humiliation, and wounding. I am inclined to think that the solution of the castration complex is simultaneously a key to the psychic integration of human destructivity and its psychoanalytic understanding. To illustrate this question, I shall present an analytic session from the third year of the analysis of a woman I will call Helen.

Helen's transference

My analysand was in her forties and the mother of three children. She had sought psychoanalytic help for her depressive moods and recurrent panic attacks. Toward the end of the third year of analysis, she already had a preliminary understanding of her penis envy and her castration impulses in the transference. We had also dealt primarily with her early psychic trauma, which was related to her mother giving birth to a stillborn baby when Helen was one year and four months old. The six months before this session had been a critical phase, during which we succeeded in working through a strong fear of annihilation. An important part of working through her panic was played by my interpretation that her desperate attacks against my separate psychic existence in the transference implied a fear of castration. Helen's next association evoked a delivery room, and a baby being born on firm ground as separate from the mother's body. No terror of being hurled endlessly into space was connected with this phantasy, as previously.

At the beginning of the session, Helen told me she had been losing many important memo-slips. She had been looking for one of them frantically, not only with her eyes, but also with her hands, groping, as if she could not trust her eyes alone. She had also thought that somebody had hidden a slip to tease her. Just before, I had moved my office to a temporary address, and asked her whether she felt that my intention was to tease her. She immediately recalled that I had given her my new address on a piece of paper that she had regarded as an important symbol of the continuity of her analysis.

Helen returned to the memo slip she had lost and said: 'I finally found this piece of paper by feeling with my hands, although I must have seen it before that. Touching with your hands feels somehow more convincing. . . . If I lose something it feels like a reversal of reality. As if things just vanished into thin air; and sometimes there's a chaotic feeling, too. As a child, I never found anything I had lost, but asked my mother to find them.'

I said that a little girl lacks a penis. Helen responded: 'Incredible! It can't be true that it isn't there . . . the very same reversal of reality. Appears to be true but can't be.' When I said that perhaps a child is then looking for something else, she proceeded, 'It feels better than groping around in emptiness. Just before you mentioned the penis, I thought about my handbag. In the beginning of the analysis, I always had to have it with me. Now it's in the car outside with your address slip in it.' I asked if this piece of paper could unconsciously signify the penis I had given her, a scant reminiscence of something originally belonging to the father.

She went on: 'Obviously it's better than nothing, and yet it does not convince me very much. Besides, I keep losing it all the time. It's not mine . . . its separateness is too obvious, I'm sorry to say. I have to believe that I can do without it. However, the idea of my handbag being stolen no longer seems like a catastrophe, as I felt in the beginning of the analysis. It would be awkward, but not the end of the world. At first, I thought that it's not possible to live without a penis.'

Freud believed that a human being probably never becomes completely free of the feeling of confusion caused by the sight of the female sexual organ, suggesting that our relation to reality is inherently marked by splitting. Correspondingly, the transformation of the *pleasure-ego* into the *reality-ego* is in all its painfulness a lifelong process which is linked to the dismantling of the fetish and the healing of the ego-split. In fact, I am inclined to believe that the ego exists *in statu nascendi*, as it were, in those areas where relinquishing the fetish leaves room for recognising the realities of life and transforming the ego so it is consonant with the perceived reality (Salonen, 1986). This process of expanding the ego, which perhaps contains an aspect of primary identification, forms the foundation for a living, constantly renewed relation to reality. Despite all its painfulness, the psychic integration of the unconscious idea of castration is a preferable alternative to inner stagnation.

Psychic integration of castration anxiety

We will understand the character of castration anxiety more clearly if we consider Max Schur's (1966) notion that from the viewpoint of the infant's rudimentary ego, the id, with its archaic ideational contents, belongs to the 'outside world', since it is located outside the perceptual apparatus in the same manner as the external reality. These two different domains of perceived reality have a further point of similarity, in that they both only gradually receive psychic representations, in tandem with maturation and psychic development, at the same time that they begin to be experienced inwardly.

My approach to the origins of the idea of castration allows us to understand how this part of human inheritance, rooted in the id, takes on individual meanings on the secondary process level from generation to generation. In this context, I cannot help thinking that decoding the genetic message attached to the idea of castration and internalising this message on the individual level is a task every generation has to perform. In terms of cultural development, too, this task is of major importance.

My starting point was that the parents' unconscious minds contain the idea of castration, and that the infant grasps it by means of id-perception, experiencing it as a real danger in this phase. The success with which the parents have resolved their drive conflicts – in this case how well they have integrated their castration anxiety – is thus of great importance. But however successful the parents' solutions may be, this does not eliminate the fact that the child evokes the castration motif in the parents, compelling them to work through it once again. If the parents have failed to integrate their drive conflicts and therefore project them onto their child, there is a limited possibility for the child to internalise his conflict and to find metaphorical significances in the idea of castration. Much psychoanalytic work is needed before the analysand can clearly differentiate between his fears and the incomplete Oedipal solutions of his parents. On the other hand, once this clarity has been gained, the foundation has been laid for developing an attitude towards the parents based on respect instead of idealisation as a disguise for unresolved ambivalence.

After the Oedipal enigma has been solved, the internalisation of castration anxiety takes place, with the ego obtaining another chance, based on signal anxiety, to control the drive economy. This structural change contains in a nutshell all the preconscious wisdom the child has gained in its struggle to achieve an adult love life. The id-level idea of castration no longer poses an existential threat to the ego. In this context, it has been transformed into the metaphor for the most painful loss imaginable.

I wish to conclude this chapter by focusing on two aspects of the *reality-ego*. First, the integration of feminine castration anxiety leads, irrespective of sex, to acceptance of one's vulnerability and to an understanding that no complete safeguard against the wounding reality is possible. Relinquishing the illusion of total safety opens up the gateway to an inner vitality and creative participation in adult love life. The integration of the masculine aspect of castration anxiety means in turn not only a painful relinquishment of incestuous infantile objects but also an inner grasp on law, in the face of which there are no sovereign rulers but only ordinary mortals with the capacity to feel guilt and remorse. The internalisation of this law, related to a consolidated superego, helps the ego to acknowledge the realities of life so as to orient itself accordingly. Such an alliance with the facts of life also gives the ego strength and penetration so it can cope with its procreative task.

Note

1 This essay was read at the 10th Nordic Psychoanalytic Congress in Turku, August 1987, and published in the *Scand. Psychoanal. Rev.*, 10: 27–36 (1987). Copyright© The Psychoanalytic Societies of Denmark, Finland, Norway and Sweden, reprinted by permission of Taylor & Francis Ltd, www.tandfonline.com on behalf of The Psychoanalytic Societies of Denmark, Finland, Norway and Sweden.

References

Chasseguet-Smirgel, J. (1974). Perversion, idealization and sublimation. *Int. J. Psychoanal.*, 55: 349–357.

Chasseguet-Smirgel, J. (1985). *Creativity and Perversion*. London: Free Association Books.

Freud, S. (1913). Totem and taboo. In *The Standard Edition of the Complete Psychological Works of Sigmund Freud*, Volume XIII. London: Hogarth Press and the Institute of Psychoanalysis, p. vii–162.

Freud, S. (1924). Dissolution of the Oedipus complex. In *The Standard Edition of the Complete Psychological Works of Sigmund Freud*, Volume XIX. London: Hogarth Press and the Institute of Psychoanalysis, pp. 171–180.

Freud, S. (1926). Inhibitions, symptoms and anxiety. In *The Standard Edition of the Complete Psychological Works of Sigmund Freud*, Volume XX. London: Hogarth Press and the Institute of Psychoanalysis, pp. 75–176.

Freud, S. (1927). Fetishism. In *The Standard Edition of the Complete Psychological Works of Sigmund Freud*, Volume XXI. London: Hogarth Press and the Institute of Psychoanalysis, pp. 147–158.

Freud, S. (1938). Moses and monotheism. In *The Standard Edition of the Complete Psychological Works of Sigmund Freud*, Volume XXIII. London: Hogarth Press and the Institute of Psychoanalysis, pp. 1–138.

Freud, S. (1940a). An outline of psycho-analysis. In *The Standard Edition of the Complete Psychological Works of Sigmund Freud*, Volume XXIII. London: Hogarth Press and the Institute of Psychoanalysis, pp. 139–208.

Freud, S. (1940b). Splitting of the ego in the process of defence. In *The Standard Edition of the Complete Psychological Works of Sigmund Freud*, Volume XXIII. London: Hogarth Press and the Institute of Psychoanalysis, pp. 271–278.

Klein, M. (1928). Early stages of the Oedipus conflict. *Int. J. Psychoanal.*, 9: 167–180.

Laplanche, J. (1976). *Life and Death in Psychoanalysis*. Baltimore, MD, and London: The Johns Hopkins Univ. Press.

McDougall, J. (1974). The Psychosoma and the psychoanalytic process. *Int. R. Psychoanal.*, 1: 437–459.

McDougall, J. (1978). Primitive communication and the use of countertransference – Reflections on early psychic trauma and its transference effects. *Contemp. Psychoanal.*, 14: 173–209.

McDougall, J. (1980). *Plea for a Measure of Abnormality*. New York: Int. Univ. Press.

McDougall, J. (1986). Identifications, neo-needs and neo-sexualities. *Int. J. Psychoanal.*, 67: 19–30.

Salonen, S. (1986). On conceptual clarity in psychoanalysis. *Scand. Psychoanal. Rev.*, 9: 57–66.

Schur, M. (1966). *The Id and the Regulatory Principles of Mental Functioning*. New York: Int. Univ. Press.

4

THE RESTITUTION OF PRIMARY IDENTIFICATION IN PSYCHOANALYSIS[1]

Radical psychic trauma signifies an existential threat to an individual, the nature of which is difficult to understand without insight into the early conditions of the infant's psychic development and the earliest identification phenomena. The discussion of this topic is difficult because psychoanalytic experience in this area tends to remain fragmentary. Beyond ordinary language and the integrated psychic functioning, it is hard to find metaphors which succeed in conveying what is at stake. Such a possibility is, however, offered by the language of psychoanalytic metapsychology, owing to its organic connection with that part of psychoanalytic understanding based on solid clinical experience.

On the conditions of the primordial ego

In *Instincts and Their Vicissitudes*, Freud (1915) introduced an idea he did not fully develop later: he suggested that the original contact with reality would be an objective one. He referred in this context to the notion of the *original reality-ego*, which then becomes transformed into the *pleasure-ego* orienting itself in terms of pleasure (p. 136). This rudimentary perceptual faculty can be conceived of as a mere point of reference to reality, devoid of any dimensions. The corresponding experience of reality would then be boundless and cosmic in nature. This mode of experience connected with radical psychic trauma involves the greatest conceivable helplessness, *Hilflosigkeit,* which is the subject under discussion.

Psychic trauma is illuminated by childhood night terrors. Boundless stimulation is typical of such episodes, without the slightest element of pleasure or consolation. The child may wander around autistically until finding contact with another person – perhaps just the sound of the mother's voice brings him back to reality. After such an episode, the child may remember his experience, but will lack the words to describe it.

The rudimentary ego cannot yet be considered a psychic formation. It is for this reason difficult to approach conceptually. The individual's earliest experiences are, furthermore, not retained in memory traces and thus do not receive a psychic representation. They instead recur repetitively without the opportunity for *recognition*, corresponding to Winnicott's (1975) stage of primary unintegration. The difficulty of understanding these conditions is perhaps also due to the notion of primary narcissism that leads us to imagine that all is necessarily well in early infancy. The cosmic mode of experience I mentioned cannot be approached from this point of view; on the contrary, it occurs specifically when the infant's wellbeing is severely endangered, or later in life when the ego – to apply Sandler and Rosenblatt's (1962) concept – is left without the protection of the *representational world*.

To understand the nature of traumatic helplessness, we are greatly aided by Max Schur's (1966, p. 72n) notion that initially all perceptual stimulation is located in external reality, regardless of whether the source of stimulation lies within or outside the organism. Thus, the somatic processes and the drive-instinctual tensions having their sources in these processes, as well as the unconscious id-ideas concern in this mode of experience all as much a part of external reality as the physical environment and the still incomprehensible world of other human beings.

Eugenio Gaddini (1982, 1987) maintained that during the first weeks of infantile life, certain somatic responses occur that will form a defence against serious maternal deprivation, with the same responses later recurring in psychosomatic disorders. This defence on the frontiers of the somatic process is based on the infant learning to imitate within its body some vital functions originally related to the mother's presence. By these means, the infant produces or generates an analogical bodily stimulation to that offered by maternal intimacy. What is involved here is a precursor of mental activity which Gaddini called 'fantasies in the body'. This phenomenon can be compared to hallucinatory wish-fulfillment, although more is involved: an actual physiological stimulation is generated by the infant when confronted with overwhelming maternal deprivation. This autoerotic stimulation at the level of vital functions is a means used by the infant to avoid succumbing to extinction. In this situation, it is irrelevant whether the source of stimulation is internal or external. What is important is that the vitalising stimulation is perceived as real.

Freud (1914) posited a link between the erogeneity of the body and narcissistic libido resources. According to him, autoerotic stimulation at the bodily level attracts large quantities of narcissistic interest, which then, in forming a fixation, serves as a defence against extreme psychic trauma. However, this solution involves another kind of dead end, namely, the bypass of psychic representation. Instead of investing libidinal resources in object love and the shared human world in general, they became bound to autoerotic stimulation on the bodily level. When developing into a psychosomatic illness, this development may lead to a defensive fortification, the dismantling of which in psychoanalysis forms an agonising threat, sometimes a more severe threat than actual death from somatic illness (McDougall, 1974).

The Swedish Nobel writer Harry Martinsson has dealt with the ultimate realm of human helplessness in his *Aniara: A Review of Man in Space and Time* (1963). This long poetic sequence describes a spaceship thrown out of orbit. After this disaster, the traveller's only focus of interest and hope is a technical device, the *Mima*, which registers events taking place in the universe with full objectivity. This device necessarily brings to mind Freud's notion of the original 'reality-ego'. Only when the Mima becomes also destroyed does the Aniara, in its linear trajectory, become an endlessly falling sarcophagus for its travellers. Of particular interest is the way in which the poet describes the situation after the ship has been thrown out of orbit and when its trajectory could no longer be corrected: first there was panic, then desperation and apathy, where the visions through the Mima offered the only relief.

Martin's early agonies

I would like to refer briefly to Martin's analysis, to which we shall return extensively in Chapter 11. Martin spent the first year of his life in a children's home. After this he was cared for by his mother. He met his father for the first time during the final phase of his analysis. Despite his apparent success in life, Martin had suffered for years from the symptoms which made him come for analysis. He considered his illnesses somatic, and he had earlier sought medical advice for them. His symptoms had begun in the form of painful genital stimulation after meeting his future wife. At that time, he thought he had somehow damaged his penis.

Soon after commencing analysis, painful bodily stimulation similar to that troubling him earlier began to recur. Before long, it became evident that the agonies of the first year of his life had begun to repeat themselves in the transference. Martin's inner vitality was disappearing. In particular, his mouth region seemed lifeless. Dangerous weight loss and the cessation of beard growth contributed to the impression of a profound drive-economic emergency. At the same time, he began to smoke heavily. Furthermore, he was preoccupied with the idea of castration and described various flows in his body as real phenomena.

During the first two years of the analysis, Martin's psychic regression required him to sit in a chair instead of lying on the couch. When we agreed to use the couch, a dramatic turn took place. The autoerotic fragmentation disappeared, and he began to differentiate his experiences at a more integrated level. At the same time, the earlier 'fantasies in the body' gave way to contents with a psychic meaning. Martin felt relieved by assuming this new position, where I could no longer see his face. Previously he had been embarrassed and ashamed, as well as afraid that I would notice his erotic excitement. Related to the idea of castration, he was also afraid of the female genital, and was terrified by his thought of drowning in it. On the other hand, this fear also involved a phantasy of returning to the moment of his conception. He hoped by means of regression to find his father there.

The next advance was uncovered in his feminine longing for the absent father. After working through his conflict with his inner parents in the transference, Martin was finally able to encounter his father personally and feel compassion for his elderly mother. At this point, after the analysis had lasted five years, he wished to terminate it.

At this final stage, Martin's early trauma had increasingly taken on inner meanings: 'Being stimulated by the presence of women is just like being a child with my mother. Now she will come to take me in her arms. . . . Her lap, uncertain footsteps and my exciting longing for pleasure, enormous desire. There was no lap; I felt drowning.' And in another context: 'Yesterday I had sensations in my penis and a sense of pleasure in my heart. That's where they belong, too – not just in the penis and the legs. Now warm feelings take their place in my heart.

I feel as though I were sitting on your belly and looking at your face like my little daughter with me.'

On the primary identification

In *Beyond the Pleasure Principle*, Freud (1920) characterised psychic trauma in terms of a simple biological organism, whose outer surface forms a stimulus barrier against the 'the enormous energies at work in the external world'. If this protective shield breaks down, the organism enters a traumatic state posing a vital threat to it. According to Freud, the pleasure principle will then collapse.

Jean Laplanche (1976, p. 134) associated Freud's analogy of a living organism with the first ego formation arising in the infant's contact with another human being. This early contact, Laplanche suggested, means not only the discovery of an object but at the same time the emergence of the subject as a metaphor for the object. Laplanche called this psychic formation the *metaphorical ego*, which I am going relate to Freud's notion of primary identification.

Green (1986) developed an additional point of view with regard to the problem of primary identification, suggesting that the early maternal fusion-object leaves behind an *imago* of the mother, which later becomes a 'framing structure' for the ego and a container of representational space. Furthermore, Green proposed that the libidinal cathexis of this space forms the matrix of future cathexes as well, which comes close to my notion of the primal representative matrix beyond primal repression (Salonen, 1979). What is also important is that Green succeeded with his notion of the framing structure in integrating Bion's (1963, 1965) concept of the *container/contained* into Freud's structural theory.

I have understood Freud's analogy of the living organism in *Beyond the Pleasure Principle* (1920) to refer to the first pleasure-ego formation: that psychic configuration within which the pleasure principle will reign. This archaic configuration comes into existence in the bodily contact with the mother. It represents an elementary experience of oneself, coinciding with the outer surface of one's body. However, this configuration is not yet a self-representation but a psychic formation contributing to the ego and the framing of the future representational world, including self- and object-representations. Understood in this way, primary identification signifies a radical change in the early conditions of the rudimentary ego, enabling psychic experience to take on a spatial dimension. As a result, the ego also receives a libidinal resource at its disposal. This view is supported by Meltzer's *et al.'s* (1975) observations of autistic children, describing how the autistic mode of psychic experience evolves dimension by dimension towards a spatial mode of psychic existence.

Eugenio Gaddini (1982) made another interesting observation, recalling René Spitz's notion of the human face as the first organiser of an infant's mind (Spitz, 1965). According to Gaddini, the first self-image corresponds to a circular shape, coinciding with the experience of the infant's body in contact with the maternal surroundings limiting it, including the intra-uterine state. This shape may occur later not only in children's drawings but also in dreams occurring during psychoanalytic treatment. In these cases, this shape evokes annihilation anxiety. In fact, Gaddini derived the urge for survival from the inception of this image.

Two clinical illustrations

I would like to present two clinical episodes, illustrating the connection between primary identification and annihilation anxiety. My first patient began her session by describing vividly how she had been able to calm herself down the preceding evening: 'I was in a strange state, the same as I sometimes used to be when I was in school. My body surface felt uneven and furry, a smooth fur like a mouse.... My outer boundary felt terribly far away, maybe half a meter from my actual skin. It was oval in shape, and I was inside it.' After this experience, she had eaten some fruit and fallen asleep. Her first association was to recall that when she was a baby, she had often been left alone outside the door to sleep. The furry surface brought to mind either a toy or an animal. When I asked her if perhaps she'd had an animal toy, she recalled her teddy bear, the surface of which had been uneven like her delusion.

My second example lacks the consolation of the transitional object; rather, it expresses the horror of annihilation and the feeling of cosmic desolation. It also brings into our discussion the repetition compulsion to which we shall return. This vignette concerns the experience of a female patient under narcosis during a surgical operation, which she recalled after decades as though it had happened yesterday. It involved a circle divided into black and white sectors, revolving both around its own centre and in a receding and approaching spiral movement.

In the distance, the spiral shrank to a black point, associated with a sense of suffocating terror and sharp pain. The white sectors were associated with a voice repeating endlessly 'no-no-no . . .', the black with 'yes-yes-yes'. As the spiral receded into the distance, the latter voice pursued the former, catching up to it at the black point, which signified death.

The conditions of early trauma cannot be discussed without commenting on aggression and destructive drive phenomena, which in turn lead us back to the primal representative matrix. In fortunate cases, this matrix binds destructive drive phenomena into living connections as aggressive wishes with their aims and objects in the outside world. In less fortunate conditions, this matrix may become an element transmitting destruction, such as *erotogenic masochism* (Freud, 1924). Might this kind of pathological infiltration of aggression and hostility be connected to a special vulnerability of the first pleasure ego formation? Freud's (1910) early notion of ego-instincts seems to be pertinent in this respect.

In being unable to repair psychic trauma, the ego remains exposed to destructive drive phenomena beyond the sphere of primary identification. The breakdown of the framing structure opens the gates to cosmic stimulation and the greatest conceivable helplessness. Annihilation anxiety serves to warn against the opening of these gates, thus acting as a danger signal, protecting the pleasure principle and by the same token the entire drive economy.

Primary identification and repetition compulsion

Harold Blum (1987) called attention to the role of identification in the recovery from psychic trauma. However, his emphasis was on a more advanced level of psychic organisation, without assigning a particular role for primary identification. In my consideration, a collapse of primary identification means that the rudimentary ego is left helpless at the mercy of an alien psychic element, that is, repetition compulsion. Let us now look at the significance of this compelling force more closely, from the viewpoint of primary identification. I believe there is a specific and highly significant link between them.

Since Freud's work, there has been disagreement over the question of whether repetition compulsion can be understood as a magical-omnipotent attempt by the ego to repair psychic trauma according to the pleasure principle, or whether it must be located beyond the pleasure principle (Schur, 1966). Jonathan Cohen (1980) has found a solution to this dilemma without committing to Freud's concept of the death drive. According to Cohen, *repetition compulsion functioning* is a central regulatory principle in the area of psychic trauma, corresponding to the pleasure principle on the organised level of wish-fulfilment. Thus, repetition compulsion constitutes a basic element in the organisation of the human mind.

What then is the relation between psychic trauma, compulsive repetition, and primary identification? I think that repetition compulsion aims at the rediscovery of the primary object. It expresses an inherent tendency toward the restoration of primary identification, anchored in the foundation of psychic functioning. On the other hand, repetition compulsion also has its reverse, 'demonic' side, the endlessly repeated loss of the primary object, involving the release of inner destruction. The outcome of psychoanalytic treatment will ultimately be realised in the polarity of these two tendencies.

Once controlled, repetition compulsion becomes a motor of the psychoanalytic process. Together with drive-instinctual wishes, it also occupies the transference, involving an opportunity for recovery of primary identification as well. The special atmosphere of the psychoanalytic setting tends to activate traumatic experiences in the past and hence compulsive repetition. Instead of offering himself as an identification object proper, the analyst's role is merely to represent the principle of primary identification, creating a container or framing structure for the analytic process to evolve. To clarify my point further: the principle of a container, its image, can be rediscovered in the psychoanalytic setting representing it. This constitutes the basis for the recovery of primary identification in psychoanalysis.

Returning to Helen's case history

I would like to come back to Helen's analysis, referred to in the previous chapter. Her main symptom, a panic state, occurred in traffic, with the fear that she would be thrown into the opposite lane. This state of panic was associated with an early psychic trauma. When she was one year and four months old, her mother gave birth to a dead child, which became intertwined in Helen's primal scene.

In the third year of analysis, we succeeded in reconstructing the ideational content of her panic state. Helen recalled a childhood nightmare involving a two-dimensional metallic shape, with the absolute certainty that she was going to die. Another dream also came to her mind: 'There was a strange, revolving object, whirling around in space until it fell. It was a capsule with something alive in it, maybe a foetus. Perhaps I was that whirling object myself, and at the same time the one watching.'

In these nightmares, Helen felt that she was completely surrounded by desolate cosmic elements like the space travellers in Harry Martinsson's *Aniara* (1963) quoted above. At a later stage in the analysis, Helen had a dream which was very dreadful for her to talk about. This dream involved two-dimensional, huge human figures, to which the knowledge of someone's death was again related. I asked Helen whether an experience like this might not lie behind her fear of being flung into traffic, to which she answered: 'It's much easier to be afraid of oncoming cars than to feel the terror that the world can no longer be *recognised*.' In the following session, her panic had receded: 'The capsule has stopped revolving, or at least now it can be stopped.'

The illusion recurred once more when Helen was driving home. The revolving capsule now appeared in the windscreen of her car. This time, however, the stable image of her mother appeared between herself and the capsule. What came to her mind were childhood snapshots, in which her mother's hair was done in the same way as in this vision. Helen was also surprised at the large size of the mother image and thought it probably corresponded to the mother as seen by the infant. Furthermore, the size of the figure was the same as in the two-dimensional nightmare figures. A further detail from this vision had also remained in her mind: the parental bed, opened up, that is, her primal scene.

Two years later, when the analysis was in its termination phase, the traumatic experience of falling had taken on psychic representation. As a result, she no longer awoke in terror at a sense of falling but was able to dream about it (Green, 1977, p. 80). One such dream proved more important than the others:

'I was lying down and looking out of the window. Outside they were building something that looked like a monument of some kind. It had concentric spheres, like an onion. The construction wasn't quite finished yet, and I was afraid that the builders would fall off. I was not only inside in the room but also outside together with the builders. Otherwise what I saw was just the same view as here, from your window.' It occurred to me to ask Helen the number of concentric spheres, to which she responded with amazement: 'It's like a breast, a monument to my mother's breast. The breast is eternally part of the past.'

The next thing that came to Helen's mind was a dream she had in the early stages of analysis, with which we had dealt thoroughly at the time. In this dream, someone had fallen from a high tower and been smashed on the ground. On the upper landing of the tower there had been a plant, resembling in shape a cow's udder, which broke off and began to bleed at the same moment as the person began to fall. When this dream now came up in her associations, I referred to the mother's unfortunate pregnancy, which had occurred at a very early period in the little girl's life, and which had therefore registered as a traumatic falling. Helen responded by telling me that her mind was just at the same moment filling with a hatred for small children, continuing: 'Finally I can understand that danger and disaster are two different things.'

Helen's early psychic trauma and her related hatred had received a psychic representation in the transference. The reconstruction of her mother's breast in her dream enabled her to realise that it was herself who had survived, while the other person who fell was her mother's stillborn baby. The capsule whirling about in her desolate primal scene had been brought to a standstill.

Representing genital reality

Psychoanalysis posits that only things which have been lost externally can be recovered on the intrapsychic level; that a truthful image can be created from that which was lost, a mental representation where one's own sensuality and the original object are uniquely intertwined, creating the foundation for inner vitality. My focus has been on the coming into existence of the first integrated image, signifying possibly the *first integrated thought* as well. This psychic configuration is crucial due to its role in providing the metaphorical space for psychic experience, and at the same time the stage where the lost object finds a psychic representation. However, this configuration cannot be detached from its broader structural context. In fact, its permanence depends to a great extent on the future vicissitudes of instinctual drives and the degree of integrity with which the ego succeeds in taking cognisance of the realities of life. Ultimately, the permanence of this configuration is tested by Oedipal renunciations and their repercussions later in life.

The metaphorical space created by primary identification is a vulnerable constellation. It is threatened not only by early misfortunes but also by new dangers, *traumata de novo* (Cohen, 1980), which may signify an experiential abyss. In this case, too, the world is no longer recognisable. It is as though a familiar face had disappeared, taking with it continuity of experience and clarity of vision. In such conditions, the recovery of primary identification brings back the sense of continuity in life. Reality perception, however, does not return to its previous shape; the container of psychic representation now extends further. The ego has, as it were, been given new eyes and now perceives the familiar face in places where earlier nothing was known to exist, and where an abysmal void had opened up.

In my previous chapter, the individual's relation to reality was examined from the point of view of castration anxiety. I came to the conclusion that the ego is in the process of transformation in those areas where relinquishing the fetish leaves room for recognising genital reality. In that connection, I suggested that this process involves an aspect of primary identification. Here my aim has been to examine how the ego can, in general, maintain its integrity in the midst of the drive-instinctual dangers inevitable in life. This strength may be based on the possibility of these dangers being metaphorically contained within a framing structure created by primary identification. I believe human dignity may also be based on this configuration.

Note

1 This paper was originally published in *Scand. Psychoanal. Rev.*, 12: 102–115 (1989). Copyright© The Psychoanalytic Societies of Denmark, Finland, Norway, and Sweden, reprinted by permission of Taylor & Francis Ltd, www.tandfonline.com on behalf of The Psychoanalytic Societies of Denmark, Finland, Norway, and Sweden.

References

Bion, W. R. (1963). *Elements of Psychoanalysis*. London: William Heinemann Medical Books.

Bion, W. R. (1965). *Transformations*. London: William Heinemann Medical Books.

Blum, H. P. (1987). The role of identification in the resolution of trauma: The Anna Freud memorial lecture. *Psychoanal. Q.*, 56: 609–627.

Cohen, J. (1980). Structural consequences of psychic trauma: A new look at 'Beyond the Pleasure Principle'. *Int. J. Psychoanal.*, 61: 421–432.

Freud, S. (1910). The psycho-analytic view of psychogenic disturbance of vision. In *The Standard Edition of the Complete Psychological Works of Sigmund Freud*, Volume XI. London: Hogarth Press and the Institute of Psychoanalysis, pp. 209–218.

Freud, S. (1914). On narcissism. In *The Standard Edition of the Complete Psychological Works of Sigmund Freud*, Volume XIV. London: Hogarth Press and the Institute of Psychoanalysis, pp. 67–102.

Freud, S. (1915). Instincts and their vicissitudes. In *The Standard Edition of the Complete Psychological Works of Sigmund Freud*. Volume XIV. London: Hogarth Press and the Institute of Psychoanalysis, pp. 117–140.

Freud, S. (1920). Beyond the pleasure principle. In *The Standard Edition of the Complete Psychological Works of Sigmund Freud*. Volume XVIII. London: Hogarth Press and the Institute of Psychoanalysis, pp. 1–64.

Freud, S. (1924). The economic problem of masochism. In *The Standard Edition of the Complete Psychological Works of Sigmund Freud*, Volume XIX. London: Hogarth Press and the Institute of Psychoanalysis, pp. 155–170.

Gaddini, E. (1982). Early defensive fantasies and the psychoanalytical process. *Int. J. Psychoanal.*, 63: 379–388.

Gaddini, E. (1987). Notes on the mind – body question. *Int. J. Psychoanal.*, 68: 315–329.

Green, A. (1977). The borderline concept. In *On Private Madness*. London: The Hogarth Press and the Institute of Psychoanalysis, 1986, pp. 60–83, 80.

Green, A. (1986). The dead mother. In *On Private Madness*. London: The Hogarth Press and the Institute of Psychoanalysis, pp. 142–173. Reference to *Narcissisme vie: Narcissisme de mort*. Paris: Minuit, 1983.

Laplanche, J. (1976). *Life and Death in Psychoanalysis*. Baltimore, MD and London: The Johns Hopkins University Press.

Martinsson, H. (1963). *Aniara, a Review of Man in Space and Time*. Adapted from the Swedish by H. MacDiarmid and E. H. Schubert. London: Hutchinson Co. Ltd.

McDougall, J. (1974). The psychosoma and the psychoanalytic process. *Int. R. Psychoanal.*, 1: 437–459.

Meltzer, D., Bremner, J., Hoxter, S., Weddel, D. and Wittenberg, I. (1975). *Explorations in Autism*. London: The Donald Harris Educational Trust and Clunie Press.

Salonen, S. (1979). On the metapsychology of schizophrenia. *Int. J. Psychoanal.*, 60: 73–81.

Sandler, J. and Rosenblatt, B. (1962). The concept of the representational world *Psychoanal. Study Child*, 17: 128–145.

Schur, M. (1966). *The Id and the Regulatory Principles of Mental Functioning.* New York: Int. Univ. Press.

Spitz, R. (1965). *The First Year of Life.* New York: Int. Univ. Press.

Winnicott, D.W. (1975). *Through Paediatrics to Psychoanalysis. Int. Psychoanal. Lib.*, 100: 1–325. London: The Hogarth Press and the Institute of Psychoanalysis, pp. 149–154.

5

THE RECONSTRUCTION OF PSYCHIC TRAUMA[1]

To illuminate this topic, I will first present an episode from the termination phase of the analysis of a woman in her forties, who was seven years old when her mother died unexpectedly. Although her catastrophic loss had been dealt with extensively, a decisive breakthrough did not take place. When the termination of the treatment had already been decided, something unexpectedly occurred: the roof of my office began to leak. I could not do anything but place a newspaper under the leak. Water was dripping through the roof, monotonously and endlessly.

The damage to the concrete analytic space signified a catastrophe for the analysand. The boundary between external reality and her psychic reality was pierced by the constant sound of dripping water. For a while, she imagined that somebody had caused the leak deliberately. Soon she began to think of her parents' engaging in sexual intercourse. Compared with this present nightmare, however, her original primal scene had felt like a living experience. The next association that arose was to her mother's death. She said: 'I have been able to avoid realising her death by always seeing her alive in other people.' I asked whether the present uncanny feeling could be related to death perceived as an external reality. Her spontaneous response was: 'I prefer even a delusion to realising what is obvious. I am used to focusing my vision on the periphery to avoid seeing what is central, that my mother is dead.'

Two sessions later, the patient described her sense of inner upheaval as follows: 'It feels as if I had discovered the other hemisphere, unknown to me until now. I can now grasp death as belonging to external reality. I have always thought that reality exists only in my mind. Now I have discovered it outside myself. The dripping of water signified the inevitable intrusion of death into my mind.' Then she became sad, and she thought once again about the idea of terminating the analysis.

Her psychic upheaval signified a *catastrophic change* (Bion, 1970), the meaning of which became evident two weeks later: she was able to visualise her life against the background of death and understood that unconditional surrender to the uncanny dripping rhythm would have meant death, that is, a fusion with death and dying. She felt that the analysis and the accidental leak had entirely changed her life perspective. I said that destiny had intervened in the course of her analysis; after that she had great difficulties in expressing her thoughts. An old Christmas carol 'Again all beautiful memories are filling my mind' occurred to her. What first prevented her from talking to me was the dread of my envy of her happy memories. Finally, I could interpret that the fear of her stepmother's envy had analogically prevented her as a child from talking about precious memories of her mother. She proceeded spontaneously: 'Sorrow is like the melting away of ice. Now I can remember! My mother was buried in March. The snow was melting, and water was dripping from the eaves.'

The concept of drive-instinctual wish

Commonly, the id is thought of as being a cauldron of drive impulses, where psychic processes do not take permanent forms. Max Schur (1966) differs somewhat from this definition, maintaining that the id consists of elementary wishes with rudimentary ego aspects. For Schur, the wish is the basic unit of psychic functioning in the id. This viewpoint does not necessarily conflict with Freud's concept of the unconscious wish in the *Interpretation of Dreams* (1901), but it adds an interesting aspect to it. In fact, Freud warns us about drawing too rigid boundaries between the different functional faculties of the mind. Schur's view also clarifies Freud's somewhat cryptic notion of *id-perception*. Following Schur's reasoning, the perceptual faculty of the rudimentary ego reaches deep into the id. Thus, the primordial wishes not only manifest the drive on the unconscious level but also configure the representational world from within as a manifestation of rudimentary ego functioning: *the primal representative matrix*.

At the hypothetical beginning of psychic development, the drive tension finds an outlet through affectomotor responses. The drive-instinctual wish as a psychic entity has not yet emerged and anticipated future satisfaction is not possible. The inevitable failure of satisfaction then compels the rudimentary ego to create the first mental representations of the absent pleasure. Henceforth, the drive-instinctual wish and the pleasure principle are conjoined.

Elementary wishes transform drive tensions into psychic form. Metaphorically speaking, these wishes become interwoven into the primal representative matrix which will then constitute the representational world from within, as it were. Moreover, this matrix has an additional function, namely, buffering vital somatic functions against life-threatening conditions. The psychosomatic illness exemplifies a traumatic collapse of this shield. If elementary wish functioning became radically decathected, destructive drive phenomena and repetition compulsion would become dominant. The choice is no longer between pleasure and unpleasure: individual survival is what is at stake.

Psychic trauma does not necessarily affect reality perception; the contrary may even be true. For example, the painful necessities of life are often perceived more distinctly, which is perhaps because there is no capacity for wishful thinking and illusions to blur reality perception. The catatonic stupor offers an extreme illustration of this phenomenon. Even then, rudimentary perception may remain intact, in spite of the radical decathexis of the representational world typical of this state.

I would like to illustrate this problem by presenting a driver's experience, who, to avoid a car crash with an elk, was compelled to drive off the highway. In a few seconds, he found himself hanging upside down by his seatbelt in the darkness. In absolute silence, he then heard fragments of glass falling, one by one, with a clink from their frame. What he found most striking was the exceptional clarity of this perception: the voice of the fragments falling signified for him a shattering of his preconscious belief in his omnipotence as a driver.

Freud's (1940, p. 198) notion of id-perception refers to the individual's capacity to perceive unconscious psychic processes: that the human mind is unconsciously aware of itself at a basic level of psychic functioning. This mode of perception also applies to the ideational contents beyond primal repression without these contents ever becoming conscious as such. I refer to the logic of primal phantasies, which the instinctual drives follow in striving towards their aims and objects in the external world. The question centres on the elementary drive phenomena outside the sphere of psychic representation, which Bion (1970) called 'thoughts without a thinker' or beta-elements.

Freud (1913) linked these drive-instinctual ideas to certain deeds carried out in the prehistory of the human species by quoting Goethe: 'In the beginning was the Deed.' According to Freud, the ideas of incest, parricide, and castration belong to humankind's primal heritage. As a part of human natural endowment, they are within the reach of id-perception as actual deeds which the ego is compelled to deal with either by enacting them or by coping with them on the intrapsychic level.

Consonant with Freud's thought, Baranger *et al.* (1988) considered psychic trauma as a retroactive manifestation of castration and patricide on the id-level. In any case, psychic trauma results when these impulses cannot be dealt with on the level of drive-instinctual wishes. In successful cases, the traumatic situation will not arise at all: imminent psychic trauma is then bound into the intrapsychic conflict in terms of separation, castration, and the loss of love, that is, the instinctual dangers.

Freud (1926) emphasised the reality character of these dangers, which understandably challenges common sense. Particularly, the threat of castration, presenting itself as an actual danger for the ego, is difficult to understand on the secondary process level. I think that this danger is not only based on the child's misapprehension of adult love life. The explanation has to be sought at a more fundamental level, asking whether human sexuality is inherently threatened by drive-instinctual dangers.

When psychic trauma is under discussion one cannot bypass the primal scene, which reflects not only the child's drive-instinctual wishes but also the abysmal void opening up between the infant's comprehension and the genital reality represented by the parents coming together. On the other hand, the primal scene offers a stage for the individual to deal with one's unbound libidinal stimulation and aggression on a psychic level (Ikonen and Rechardt, 1984). Because the Oedipal desire cannot be fulfilled, the child is forced to renounce his or her sexual strivings in relation to the parents. This does not, however, signify an effacement of the original wishes entirely. What remains is authentic psychic intensity and a never-fulfilled longing for happiness, which are transposed to the future in the capacity of the ego-ideal forming a constituent part of the consolidated superego.

Identification and psychic trauma

Major identifications during the child's formative years signify a strategic leap in psychic development. This holds true for both the early identifications contributing to the emergent ego as well the later ones resulting in the consolidation of the superego. Because our interest at this point is focused on psychic trauma, the early identifications are in the foreground, especially that which Freud (1923) called *primary identification*.

Freud's notion of primary identification is somewhat ambiguous since it is linked to object finding before ordinary object ties. According to Freud, it takes place in relation to the early father or perhaps both parents, leading to the emergence of the ego-ideal. Customarily, however, we are used to relating identification to existing object ties. To overcome this conceptual ambiguity, it has been proposed that primary identification could denote early maternal fusion (Blum, 1987; Sandler and Perlow, 1987). Consequently, primary identification should not involve any psychic configuration. Freud's notion becomes more understandable in the light of Green's study (1986). According to Green, the early maternal fusion does not disappear without a trace in the process of individuation; instead, it will leave behind a kind of psychic framing structure for the ego, constituting the container of the representational space.

In the previous chapter, I examined primary identification from the viewpoint of psychic representation, which resulted in the following train of thought: In the early human environment, the mother brings a human image within reach of the infant's rudimentary perception. Primary identification leads to the establishment of this image within the infant's emerging mind as a psychic configuration, forming a frame for psychic representation. This configuration is sensory-perceptual in nature, not based on existing object ties. It is not yet a self-representation, but a configuration within the frame of which psychic representation will then be located. The capacity for psychic representation, as well as the pleasure principle, depend upon this configuration. Accordingly, psychic trauma denotes a collapse of this formation.

It is noteworthy that Freud proposed his notion of primary identification in *The Ego and the Id* (1923), where he also formulated for the first time his structural theory. In fact, the coming into existence of the early ego-ideal through primary identification represents a critical leap toward organised psychic functioning, which is even more significant if the capacity for psychic representation proves to be linked to this configuration.

Against the background of the psychoanalytic experience of radical psychic trauma, the infant's primary narcissistic wellbeing cannot be taken for granted. The early paradise is not boundless since it prevails only within limits defined by the parent's metaphorical presence. Outside this domain, psychic trauma prevails, with its desolate drive elements. Projected into the future, primary identification will configure the ego-ideal, vitalise the anticipation of future satisfaction, and outline the sphere of individual psychic integrity and wellbeing.

The psychoanalytic setting represents the same configuration as that which the parents originally bring within reach of the infant's rudimentary perception. Instead of proposing himself as an object of drive-instinctual satisfaction, the psychoanalyst's task is to take care of the psychoanalytic setting as a shared frame for psychic representation of elementary drive phenomena. This particular attitude expands the psychoanalytic space and activates the analytic instrument (Norman, 1991).

The etymology of the Finnish verb *ymmärtää*, to understand, is derived from the noun *ympyrä*, circle. It signifies drawing a circle or circumscribing something (Häkkinen, 1987). In fact, the psychoanalytic situation means shaping a frame of understanding around something that is incomprehensible and, hence, traumatic. In successful cases, this also makes the analytic solution to the intrapsychic conflict possible. The specific quality of hope characterising psychoanalysis is based on this constellation.

In examining the unconscious wish, we arrived, via the instinctual dangers, at the superego. The study of primary identification led us to the ego-ideal. Conjointly, these two structural faculties constitute the advanced conscience, enabling the ego to orient itself in the midst of the drive-instinctual dangers inevitable in life, while at the same time avoiding psychic trauma. Thus, a consolidated superego represents a significant structural achievement safeguarding the individual against psychic trauma throughout life.

Facing annihilation: a case history

Alice was a young single woman in her twenties. She had been involved in a fateful car accident at the age of sixteen, where the family's car caught fire, killing her father and leaving her mother injured, though she recovered later. Alice herself was spared physical injury, although her psychic trauma is now under my consideration.

When I met her for the first time, Alice felt depressed and miserable. She suffered from many somatic ailments, such as respiratory allergies, eczema, and headaches. Furthermore, her social contacts were progressively deteriorating. In this phase, we began a psychotherapy that lasted three years. At its termination, her life was outwardly in order. For example, she had started her academic studies. Simultaneously, however, Alice realised that the solutions found were still unsatisfactory and that she would possibly need psychoanalysis in future.

When the analysis began a year and a half later, a new problem emerged that had not appeared during the psychotherapy. Alice had special difficulty linking mental images to words and sentences. Now and then, her thoughts remained incomplete, in a precursory stage. The problem was not a lack of capacity for conceptual thinking; rather, the contrary.

Many somatic sensations and troubles characterised this initial phase of her analysis. Alice's phobic symptoms were also accentuated. She was terrified of small animals, mainly insects. Now and then, she would sit on the couch for a while, to pull herself together. Although her associations were often fragmentary and incoherent, she was never psychotic. My feelings from this period illuminate what was going on in the analytic process. Very often, I could not find any point in what I had heard, which felt bewildering. Furthermore, I began to descend into a somnolent state from which it was tough to extricate myself. In fact, I had to make significant efforts to hold on to the actual meaning of our work. To rescue at least some material from falling into ultimate oblivion, I occasionally began to take notes during the sessions. The analysis proceeded following the logic of very early psychic processes.

During the first year of her analysis, Alice frequently sank into a desolate state of experience that alternated between uncontrollable shivering with colds and headaches. She imagined living on a lonely island and was afraid that I would take away this last place of refuge. It is important to mention that the sea and shore, in general, played a major role in her associations, which also refer to the earliest stages of the individual psychic development (Winnicott, 1967).

When the analysis proceeded, fantasies related to primary narcissistic perfection came explicitly to the fore: 'Words destroy this completeness because they are incomplete. No voice is related to this state of mind. My island has shrunk into now being a tiny rock, and you are no longer present. Deep waters and darkness surround me. It sounds peculiar, but I am not freezing; it feels warm. One cannot compare this perfection with anything.'

Some months later, Alice began to shape in her mind fragments of a circle, without, however, being able to link them together. When at last she succeeded in this endeavour, she emphasised that it was not a handmade circle she was shaping, but the circle's coming into existence. In the same session, she was able for the first time to describe her fragmentary self-experience: Alice experienced her limbs as detachable, and her thoughts as disconnected, placed outside her mind. What was going on in the analytic setting was the recovery of the same psychic configuration that Eugenio Gaddini (1987) designated as the *basic mental organisation* and which I have linked to the primary identification.

When the analysis continued, Alice's uncontrolled freezing and her longing for peaceful wellbeing seemed to be interrelated. Because she was born in winter, I asked her whether she had slept outdoors as a baby. Alice responded by relating that she had asked her mother the same question the day before. In fact, she had become preoccupied with a yellow colour without being able to explain it. According to her mother, Alice had been sleeping outdoors, in a yellow cover. During the same session, she told me that her insect phobia was disappearing. At that time, Alice was more fascinated by insects than repelled by them. She fantasised about their crushing mandibles without falling into panic as before.

The analysis evolved like an ascending spiral around her traumatic experience. In this phase, the car accident was predominantly associated with oral-aggressive themes: the devouring mouths and crushing jaws, signifying jaws of death. On the other hand, she described the accident extremely 'objectively' without any particular affect tone. Even the background noise of psychic processes felt silenced: 'My father was dead, and my mother was unconscious. Time had come to a standstill. What was left was the knowledge that I will die by burning. I saw only yellow and red colours; the flames that I knew should kill me. I could not hear anything, not smell either. . . . All the time I was aware of what had happened.'

Strange bodily sensations reflect an autoerotic fragmentation. At the end of the second year of analysis, Alice felt a strange twitching in her arm, which disappeared immediately when she was able to invoke a consoling fantasy or image from her day-care home as a child. She could say: 'I would like to return to those images, for living outside them feels like a nightmare, I feel surrounded by coldness. I have dropped into cold reality. If it becomes still colder, I am not sure if I am willing to understand anymore.' In referring to her suicidal impulses, she once said: 'Deceitful death pretends to be warm although it is ice-cold.'

The idea of castration frequently occurred in the analytic material. In the beginning, it concerned the fragmented bodily experience: 'I would like to cut my bad foot off, but the idea of a stump feels awful. It would, however, be yet more horrible if the stump would be opened up. Then all the bones, tendons and muscles would become visible. They do not function as a whole, but disjointedly.' On the other hand, Alice had already found a way out of these fragmented sensations and destructive fantasies: 'I am now thinking about the dune as a geographic formation. Its cross-section is beautiful, and there is nothing incomprehensible in it. The consistency of the dune feels wonderful in one's hand, and its shape is perfect.' In the dune, she was able to grasp, metaphorically, her mother's breast as a solid psychic formation referring to the ego-ideal.

After two years of analysis, Alice made an important observation. She realised that she had been seeking a miserable life. In this connection, for the first time, I could interpret her anxiety as the result of intrapsychic conflict and unconscious guilt. She spontaneously responded: 'I resist recovery with every cell of my body.' In the following session, however, she was amazed at the consequences of my interpretation. She wondered how technically dividing the mind into different parts could have such far-reaching consequences. From then on, Alice was able to enjoy her studies instead of experiencing them as analogous to a forced labour camp, as before. The change of technical perspective indicated that a preliminary mastery of psychic trauma had been attained. The destructive repetition compulsion and her passionate addiction to suffering – her erotogenic masochism (Freud, 1924) – little by little yielded to more advanced psychic functioning according to the pleasure principle. Consequently, a structural interpretation of psychic conflict in the transference became possible.

Alice's intrapsychic conflict was accentuated by the progress of her academic studies. Her Master's thesis, for example, became associated with her Oedipal desire for the dead father represented by her analyst in the transference.

In this phase, the car accident took on the meaning of castration in her mind: 'I would like to scream like a child submitting to the taking of a blood test. Never! It feels horrible. I think that this room could be a terrifying place on earth. I refuse to recognise the awful instruments. The whole idea is only buzzing in my head. I do not understand anything!'

When the analysis then continued, psychic trauma was dealt with predominantly in terms of anality: 'My head feels stuffy. I would like to get rid of all the mess that fills up my mind. I would like to have clear thoughts.' When Alice recognised her angry feelings toward me, the atmosphere in the sessions was clarified, and she could understand that her headache was connected to her aggression. In this phase, she also dreamt of giving birth to a living baby instead of dead one, which she had dreamt before. Alice could now remember having totally lost her sleeping rhythm at the beginning of psychotherapy, after becoming conscious of her destructive thoughts towards her little godchild. At that time, she had been completely incapable of dealing with her internal aggression without becoming deeply disturbed.

Slowly, Alice came to understand that her psychic catastrophe was connected with identification with her dead father. She was horrified by her thought of being buried alive. After this idea had become conscious, she suffered from intensive headaches, and her eczema also reappeared. Alice thought that these symptoms represented an ultimate endeavour to avoid the worst possible: 'When it is most horrible, I feel like a point. All that is awful surrounds me.' Thus, she had found a metaphorical expression for her extreme helplessness, an existence without dimensions. In fact, Alice had arrived at the mathematical definition of the point: a location in space, devoid of any dimensions.

Only when Alice became conscious of her aggressive thoughts and hatred towards me in the transference could she experience my bodily presence as real: 'I don't like it at all that you are becoming more and more of a human being. I had much more liking for the voice and ear only. You get on my nerves more and more. After leaving this room, I have lately been filled with rage.' And then: 'What an unbelievable springtime, I don't have any allergic symptoms at all!' Respiratory symptoms had been persecuting her every spring since the car accident. Towards the end of the session, I reverted to her dislike about my body. She replied: 'Forget it. Let's put it into a coffin and nail the lid tightly. Let's bury it so deep that it can never be found.'

At the beginning of the following session, Alice was embarrassed by the intensity of her burial fantasy. She then proceeded: 'I am now shaping a state of perfection. I am living within a ball which is surrounded by lovely things. The wind is whistling through the trees, and it is warm. You have free access to my ball. Perhaps that's why I feel so secure.' After a silence of ten minutes, she said: 'When I just came out of the ball, the sense of time came back, and it feels no longer as comfortable as before. It is peculiar, but I was thinking about the burying of coffins just before the ball occurred to me, and now I am thinking about it again.' Time and the great negative of life, death, were waiting outside her early paradise to be dealt with on the metaphorical level in the transference.

Alice's vision of the ball corresponded to the archaic shape Gaddini has described and that I have related to primary identification. Within this configuration, the metaphorical representation of elementary drive phenomena becomes possible. Doubtless, the pleasure principle is also connected with this configuration, and outside psychic trauma prevails. Alice was for the first time able to share this space with me, which represented the reverse of her desolate island at the beginning of her analysis.

When Alice's analysis proceeded, her particular difficulty with linking mental images to words and sentences was dealt with in terms of separation: 'I have a thought, but I am unable to formulate it ... this feels peculiar, but I cannot bind it together. There are two parts: one is a tiny tot under the blanket, and the other is the coming weekend.' I asked if her inchoate thought could be of such an early origin that her capacity for binding its parts together was not yet developed, and as a result of this, the tiny tot and the separation from me, that is the coming weekend, could not be linked together. Alice went on: 'I can't catch it. I have ... perhaps it is an image of an invisible ball the diameter of which is one and a half meters. One can cling to the surface of this ball. The sensation was at first only in my hands, but now I feel it in my whole body.'

A week later, we were able to reconstruct the car accident in terms of traumatic separation from me in the transference: 'I wonder if I would still be ready to depart from life as easily as at that time. The situation was definitively hopeless. I can't be sure whether I would like to cling to life tooth and claw now either ... I am afraid that I would not survive it another time. Dying is extremely easy.' Then the thoughts of the approaching summer holidays occurred to her and in particular an Arctic voyage she was embarking on in two weeks with her mother: 'It is easy to think about drowning. The awful mouths would be there waiting in the sea, or, perhaps I would die by freezing, floating in the life jacket . . . I am now afraid that something dangerous would happen to you during the holidays.'

Alice was relieved when she appeared at the following session: 'I have the feeling that some black beast has disappeared. Can you explain this?' My explanation was an analytic reconstruction: she was no longer exposed to the experience of inner death defenceless, as previously. On the contrary, I suggested that she was afraid of being unable to maintain her inner tie to me during the holiday break, to which she responded spontaneously: 'That sounds plausible . . . Is it now over?' When the summer holidays then began, she was confident of coping with the feeling of separation from me. For the first time during the analysis, she was able to experience separation as a painful loss instead of an imminent catastrophe.

In coming back in the autumn, Alice was eager to tell me she had succeeded in keeping me alive in her mind during the holiday break. From this stage on, the character of her six-year analysis changed. Libidinal wishes and anxieties related to the Oedipus complex were then in the foreground. However, while taking her final examination before graduating, she felt, once again, on the verge of an inner catastrophe, for failing the examination would have signified the loss of her father's love in relation to me in the transference.

Alice had never discussed the car accident with her mother because she could not believe that her mother had understood her ambivalence in facing death and dying. The mother herself had been in a comatose state in the burning car. Also, Alice lacked the words to talk about the disaster to anybody. In discussing this problem, she said: 'You once asked me whether nature felt dead after my father's death. It is important because nature was our great mutual interest. Nature, however, was not entirely dead, for I have been able to find a new interest in it through my studies.' Alice was speaking not only about the recovery of her primary object, represented here by Nature, but also about her ambivalent love toward her father, reconstructed in the transference, which partly explained her profound addiction to suffering as a defence against the psychic integration and the work of mourning.

Note

1 The paper was first read at *the 13th Nordic Psychoanalytic Congress*, Reykjavik, July 1992, and published *Scand. Psychoanal. Rev.*, 12: 102–115,

(1992). Copyright© The Psychoanalytic Societies of Denmark, Finland, Norway, and Sweden, reprinted by permission of Taylor & Francis Ltd, www.tandfonline.com on behalf of The Psychoanalytic Societies of Denmark, Finland, Norway, and Sweden.

References

Baranger, M., Baranger, W. and Mom, J. M. (1988). The infantile psychic trauma from us to Freud: Pure trauma, retroactivity and reconstruction. *Int. J. Psychoanal.*, 69: 113–128.

Bion, W. R. (1970). *Attention and Interpretation*. London: William Heineman Medical Books Ltd.

Blum, H. P. (1987). The role of identification in the resolution of trauma: The Anna Freud memorial lecture. *Psychoanal. Q.*, 56: 609–627.

Freud, S. (1901). The interpretation of dreams. In *The Standard Edition of the Complete Psychological Works of Sigmund Freud*, Volume IV (1900): The interpretation of dreams (First Part). London: Hogarth Press and the Institute of Psychoanalysis, pp. ix-627.

Freud, S. (1913). Totem and taboo. In *The Standard Edition of the Complete Psychological Works of Sigmund Freud*, Volume XIII. London: Hogarth Press and the Institute of Psychoanalysis, p. vii-162.

Freud, S. (1923). The ego and the id. In *The Standard Edition of the Complete Psychological Works of Sigmund Freud*, Volume XIX. London: Hogarth Press and the Institute of Psychoanalysis, pp. 1–66.

Freud, S. (1924). The economic problem of masochism. In *The Standard Edition of the Complete Psychological Works of Sigmund Freud*, Volume XIX. London: Hogarth Press and the Institute of Psychoanalysis, pp. 155–170.

Freud, S. (1926). Inhibitions, symptoms and anxiety. In *The Standard Edition of the Complete Psychological Works of Sigmund Freud*, Volume XX. London: Hogarth Press and the Institute of Psychoanalysis, pp. 75–176.

Freud, S. (1940). An outline of psycho-analysis. In *The Standard Edition of the Complete Psychological Works of Sigmund Freud*, Volume XXIII. London: Hogarth Press and the Institute of Psychoanalysis, pp. 139–208.

Gaddini, E. (1987). Notes on the mind – body question. *Int. J. Psychoanal.*, 68: 315–329.

Green, A. (1986). The dead mother. In *On Private Madness*. London: The Hogarth Press and the Institute of Psychoanalysis, 142–173. Reference to *Narcissisme vie: Narcissisme de mort*. Paris: Minuit, 1983.

Häkkinen, K. (1987). *Nykysuomen Sanakirja 6*. Porvoo: Werner Söderström Osakeyhtiö.

Ikonen, P. and Rechardt, E. (1984). On the universal nature of primal scene fantasies. *Int. J. Psychoanal.*, 65: 63–72.

Norman, J. (1991). The analytic frame, theatrical understanding, and interpretation in child analysis. *Scand. Psychoanal. Rev.*, 14: 139–155.

Sandler, J. and Perlow, M. (1987). Internalization and externalization. In *Projection: Identification and Projective Identification*. Sandler, J. (editor). London: Karnac Books.

Schur, M. (1966). *The Id and the Regulatory Principles of Mental Functioning*. New York: Int. Univ. Press.

Winnicott, D. W. (1967). Location of cultural experience. In *Playing and Reality*. Harmondsworth: Penguin Books, 1974, p. 112.

6

THE RECOVERY OF AFFECT AND STRUCTURAL CONFLICT[1]

The impetus for this chapter was furnished by an ordinary analytical hour when I found myself saying to the analysand at the end of her session that hate and destruction were not the same phenomena. I had realised that her feeling hate did not present the slightest danger to her; however, the same could not be said about her past acting-out behaviour, indicating the dispersal of her solid affect experience. A more comprehensive process of integration became evident in what my patient said at the beginning of the following session: 'Upon leaving yesterday, I thought you looked sad. I also realised that you are a separate individual. I am not sure whether the sorrow was my own or yours, but I felt that you can contain it without it interfering with your listening.'

On affect integration

The unconscious ideational content of the instinctual drive and the concomitant affect response constitute an integrated whole. However, in the case of psychic trauma this experiential entity may break down. If the capacity for psychic representation fails, the solid affect experience tends to disperse into diffuse bodily excitation and disconnected id-impulses. Instead of emerging as object-directed wishes, the instinctual drive then seeks discharge as a direct action, whereas the concomitant affect response approximates the bodily processes or becomes entirely re-somatised (Schur, 1955, 1966). I am going to illustrate this topic with a second clinical example.

I had been treating Eric, a man in his sixties, for many years in psychotherapy without his psychotic depression improving. An unrealistic sense of guilt, sadomasochistic misery, and diffuse aggression characterised not only his inner world but also his relationship with his wife. An unexpected change took place in Eric's condition after witnessing President Anwar Sadat's assassination on television. This violent incident momentarily restored his normal psychic functioning; however, Eric experienced another problem. He could hardly sleep during the following nights because he was frightened by the thought of killing his wife. Being confronted with the idea of killing resulted in his becoming capable of experiencing the respective affect response. In this context, it is important to mention that Eric's mother had suffered from tuberculosis throughout his childhood years and died when he was an adolescent. This partly explains why his intimate object ties were to remain extremely ambivalent, as was his relationship with his wife.

Eric's psychotic mood reflected a dispersed affect state and a broken capacity for psychic representation of destructive drive phenomena. A diffuse negative affect infiltrated his mind until he unexpectedly entertained the idea of killing. His drastic recovery was not only related to a vicarious release of his aggression through projective identification with President Sadat's assassin, but also indicated a re-integration of his collapsed affect experience.

André Green (1977) maintained that pathological affect infiltrations are related to the fact that the child's psychic apparatus registers the memory traces of affects before it is capable of establishing memory traces of ideational perceptions. As a result, supplying the content to what is already experienced in unrepresentable form is a fundamental task of the psychic apparatus. If this process fails, we are confronted with inarticulate affect infiltrations typical of psychic trauma.

Bodily dimension of affects

Not only human sexuality but also affects evolve from bodily intimacy between infant and mother (Laplanche, 1976; McDougall, 1985). Perhaps contrary to all expectations, mental perception also relies on bodily responses. In analysing the problem of primary identification, Otto Fenichel arrived at this insight:

> Stimulus intake and stimulus discharge, perception and motor reaction stand extraordinary close together; they are inseparably

interwoven. Primitive perception is precisely characterised by its closeness to motor reaction. One perceives by first changing one's body through the influence of the perceived object – and then taking cognizance of this bodily change.

(1946, p. 36)

Fenichel's insight applies not only to the infant at the inception of psychic development but also to advanced human interaction. We perceive the delicate nuances of interaction with other people through our affectomotor responses, faster than our conscious thoughts. Normally, drive-instinctual ideation and spontaneous bodily responses are consonant, but if this fails the ego is left without an important reference for reality. This becomes still more understandable when we take signal anxiety into consideration, which is an integrated affect response to drive-instinctual dangers. At this point the dissociation of the bodily link signifies that the entire psychic regulation may become endangered.

Eugenio Gaddini (1992) took Fenichel's idea of affectomotor perception as his starting point. According to Gaddini, human mental organisation cannot only be derived from the *oral-introjective area* of infantile experience, but also from the *psychosensory area*. At this point, Gaddini's metapsychological thinking differs from Kleinian theory, which takes the early oral-introjective phantasies as its starting point.

Gaddini further suggested that certain somatic responses active in early infancy may play a defensive role later in life. He came to this conclusion, together with Renata Gaddini, in their early study of rumination related to serious maternal deprivation (Gaddini and Gaddini, 1959). These authors had observed that three-month-old children are already able to imitate within their body the genuine feeding experience by inducing respective physiological changes in their alimentary system. Gaddini (1982) characterised these kinds of self-induced physiological phenomena as 'fantasies in the body'. These forerunners of defence do not disappear without a trace in the course of psychic development but can be reactivated later in life – for example, in the form of hypochondriac sensations or psychosomatic manifestations. In this case, they have a twofold defensive function: they shield the helpless ego from annihilation and they form a pathological fixation hampering psychic integration.

Many psychotic phenomena can also be related to these kinds of bodily excitation. The schizophrenic hallucinations which are often incorrectly analogised with dreams are one such example. Whereas the dream represents normal psychic functioning that follows the pleasure principle, the schizophrenic hallucination represents a self-induced pathological excitation aimed at restoring a fragmented sense of being. I have in mind a catatonic woman who exemplified the difference between normal dreaming and psychotic hallucination. She became extremely frightened of her dreams after recovering normal psychic functioning during her treatment: 'I am more horrified by my dreams which I feel are alive than by my hallucinations which I can control.'

Although the infant's primordial affect responses hardly receive discernible ideational contents, this realm of the psychic experience is crucial in forming a vital foundation for more differentiated affect states. Heikki Piha's study of the non-lexical messages of spoken language shed additional light on this subject. He was able to show that the sonorous aspect of speech can communicate very subtle feeling states and affect tones that become perceived only by way of bodily perception. In fact, Piha derived the capacity for intuition from early bodily interaction between the infant and its mother (Piha, 1985, 2005).

Drive dimension of affects

Otto Kernberg (1984, 1994) conceived of affects as the primary motivational system which becomes supraordinated by drives and wish formation.

> Having explained how I see the relation between drives and affect, I hasten to add that drives are manifest not simply by affects, but by the activation of a specific object relation, which includes an affect in which the drive is represented by a specific desire or wish. Unconscious fantasy, the most important being oedipal in nature, includes a specific wish directed toward an object. The wish derives from the drive and is more precise than the affect state, an additional reason for rejecting the concept that would make affects rather than drives the hierarchically supraordinate motivational system.
>
> (1984, p. 237)

In my discussion, the compelling urge to realise primal phantasies constitutes the impetus of the instinctual drive. Only secondarily, this urge becomes represented at the level of the wish. On the other hand, the remotest part of the ego remains in touch with these elementary drive phenomena without their ever becoming conscious. In normal psychic functioning they remain beyond primal repression (Freud, 1915). The instinctual drive receives affective meaning when its ideational aspect and the concomitant bodily excitation coalesce in the infant's sensual interaction with its parents, with the evolving object ties constituting the platform for this unification.

Veikko Tähkä (1993) suggested that the emergence of affects is closely related to self – object differentiation. According to Tähkä, the negative affects related to aggression do not emerge until the capacity for the psychic representation of frustration becomes possible after self – object differentiation. The affect quality of aggression represents the way in which the evolving self, differentiated from the object, experiences accumulating drive tension, both as an affect state and an impetus to action. According to Tähkä, affects are crucial carriers of subjective meanings, while at the same time functioning like a barometer in the regulation of psychic experience. However, psychic meanings cannot emerge and be sustained only on the basis of affect responses and drive-instinctual urges. What is also required for establishing living psychic experience is language, which forms the commonly shared context for preconscious meanings. The collapse of this link is typical of schizophrenic fragmentation, in which bizarre neologisms have replaced the natural language.

Schizoaffective repercussions of a childhood sexual trauma

I met Beatrice for the first time in the 1960s when she had fallen ill with a schizoaffective psychosis in the closing phase of her academic studies. We started psychotherapy after her admission to the mental hospital where I was working as a resident at that time. Her treatment continued for eight years, mainly meeting three times a week. Later on, we met occasionally whenever she needed psychotherapeutic help. Some twenty years ago, she contacted me again after her psychic coherence had begun to disintegrate, relating to her menopause.

Falling in love initially presented a stumbling block for Beatrice and repeatedly resulted in psychotic fragmentation with confused affect states. This was related to sexual traumatisation in her latency years, as a consequence of which she had great difficulties in containing her sexual arousal later in life. Her relationship to reality broke down, and her speech deteriorated into a puzzle of loose associations. In the later phases of her illness, she also had auditory hallucinations, which only afterwards could be reconstructed as dissociated superego demands.

The first three years of Beatrice's treatment were characterised by recurring outbursts of affect and violent behaviour, alternating with a collapse of her inner vitality reminiscent of hebephrenic psychosis. To describe how this phase was brought under control, I shall select some sessions, which of course have to be considered against the background of all the transference–countertransference difficulties familiar to psychoanalysts who have treated schizophrenic patients on the transference–countertransference basis (Searles, 1965; Salonen, 1976; Pao, 1979; Volkan, 1995).

In one session Beatrice was chatting to her mirror image thus: 'You are dead to life. Finally, I can understand that I am dead. To sleep for beautiful dreams is not life, to sleep is to be awakened in emptiness, again and again. I am close to realising something. It feels safe. Perhaps this is a good starting point.'

Some days later, she returned to her hopeless situation: 'I feel that all my energy is dammed up in my legs and arms, but it does not extend to my chest at all. Something is tied up in my chest.' I asked whether it could be her anger. Unexpectedly, Beatrice went into an incredible fit of rage, which was discharged by violent force. Because it was a plain manifestation of affect without any intention of causing injury to me, I felt safe. After recovering from this fit, she was free from her distress. She said: 'The emptiness has gone. . . . It sounds peculiar, but also the heavy lump in my chest has disappeared . . . I feel powerful.'

Half a year later we returned to the same theme, just at the time Beatrice was planning to leave the hospital. This session was reminiscent of child analysis. She began playfully: 'Now, I have a delusion of a solid little girl sitting here, beside myself. She is made of solid flesh, not of alternate layers of air and flesh like I feel myself to be.' I asked her where might the lump then be hiding. She said: 'There outside, within some hollow tree trunk, or perhaps in this room beside me. . . . The lump seems to be a very stubborn and angry one, precisely like I used to be before falling ill . . . I think that the little one will take charge of my life from now on.'

This piece of analytic work demonstrates how the psychic integration of anger may form a decisive step towards experiencing one's body as solid and alive, and, conversely, how the dispersal of this affect may result in a fatal drive-economic emergency. On the other hand, the close connection between affect integration and self-object differentiation is evident in Beatrice's fantasy about the lump within the hollow tree having been transformed into a solid little girl.

Nonetheless, Beatrice's psychic coherence became fragmented again, and she lapsed into a state of profound apathy, lasting several months. This state was also revealed in her bodily appearance. In this phase, her Oedipal wishes came openly to the fore in the transference. When the treatment seemed to have completely stagnated, I came to think that castration anxiety could obstruct the therapeutic process, which was subsequently confirmed.

All kinds of trinkets and cosmetics had been disappearing in the ward, and the nursing staff had their suspicions. When Beatrice came to her next session, I asked her if she had ever wished to be a boy or perhaps imagined herself having lost a penis. Without hesitation, she told of having had such a wish. She had also imagined that her mother had torn her penis from her. When she came to the next session, I asked if she perhaps had stolen the trinkets in the ward to supply herself with a penis. Instantly, she opened her bag and poured all the pilfered things on the couch. From this point on, Beatrice's Oedipal constellation slowly began to take shape in her treatment.

Five years later, Beatrice was able to fall in love without psychotic fragmentation. She recollected then her childhood sexual fantasies, which had been related to her father and then attached to her brother. Discussing her masturbation in adolescence, she said: 'The void has now disappeared. Earlier, all living connections were damaged. There were only disconnected blocks. I was unable to construct them in any way I wanted; it all only became built.' Referring to the psychotic fragmentation of her language, Beatrice went on: 'Then my mind was replaced by the language.' Without knowing psychoanalytic theory more closely, she concluded her train of association by saying: 'My trauma was that I got excited as a child without finding any permissible discharge.'

Contacting me some years later, Beatrice was experiencing great difficulties because her psychic coherence was once again in danger. She told of having auditory hallucinations and was worried about her beautiful home, which she imagined had been deliberately damaged. She was living alone in her childhood home after her parents' death over ten years ago. She was especially worried about an antique tile stove. We had been analysing the same delusion for many years, proceeding on the notion that the stove represented Beatrice's body, which she thought had been damaged by her traumatic experience as a child.

This time, the imminent psychotic fragmentation was brought under control in a few weeks by Beatrice being hospitalised. When we met the next time, after the hospital treatment, I was preoccupied by a particular question: is it possible that after the structural consolidation attained during Beatrice's long psychotherapy her symptoms would in the first place disclose a hysterical conflict? Another patient of mine had given me occasion to pose this question some weeks before. She also had a long period of psychotherapy behind her, after having fallen ill with a catatonic psychosis in her twenties. She told me her catatonic stupor had been analogous to the present situation, with the difference that the object of her sexual wishes had then been her father instead of me in the transference.

To return to Beatrice, upon entering my office she was euphoric, and her associations were scattered in a way familiar to both of us. After first commenting on her stay in the hospital, she began to chat about the renovations going on in her house. Her grandfather, a successful businessman at the beginning of the last century, had built the house. When he had died, Beatrice's mother was only four years old.

Beatrice returned to her cherished stove, which she thought had been damaged by the bricklayer. Then a remarkable change took place. She told me she had been full of sorrow the day before, related to a feeling of painful disillusionment with her beloved brother. The endless disputes over her grandfather's estate added to this disillusionment. Also, she had been informed the day before of her uncle's death. Then Beatrice said:

'Nothing is left of the grand family. It took so long for me to understand that my mother was only four years old when her father died. That is why the illusion of her father's grandiosity was so badly needed. You said once that nobody could evade renouncing one's omnipotence. I must say that this summer I have been compelled to accept my own weakness, and strength.' I then brought up the renovations in her grandfather's house and asked whether the antique stove and perhaps also the house, in general, represented her grandfather's phallus for her. She proceeded: 'Exactly right. This session has been a deciphering of the riddle . . . a great conclusion.'

Whereas the vignette of President Anwar Sadat's assassination led us to the crossroads of Thebes where King Oedipus came to kill his father, Beatrice's case highlights another aspect of the Oedipus complex, namely the riddle of the Sphinx, which refers to the child's fusional image of the omnipotent pre-Oedipal mother. Only after renouncing her belief in her mother's phallic omnipotence was Beatrice capable of facing the painful realities of her life and feeling the sorrow.

The structural point of view

In her review of psychoanalytic theories of affect, Ruth Stein (1999) maintained that structural theory has tended to estrange psychoanalysis from emotional experience, which explains why the affect has not been the central focus of Freudian psychoanalysis. According to her, Kleinian theory takes the opposite approach: it takes the passionate feelings of love and hate as its starting point without, however, analysing them from a structural point of view. In resolving this dilemma, Stein gave special recognition to Joseph Sandler, who was able to integrate the experiential sphere of the human mind into structural theory through his concept of the *representational world* (Sandler and Rosenblatt, 1962). According to Stein, André Green's contribution is also of great importance, showing that not only the instinctual drives but also the affects receive an unconscious psychic representation.

According to Green (1986), the early maternal object of fusion leaves behind a framing structure that comes to form the container for the emerging psychic representations. Gaddini (1982) described an analogical psychic configuration that I have related to Freud's notion of primary identification. This configuration, psychosensory in nature, comes into existence by means of the infant finding another human being and, simultaneously, himself as a metaphor of the other, corresponding to Laplanche's (1976) notion of the metaphorical ego. With certain relevant reservations, primary identification can be compared to the ethological imprinting of animal offspring, which underlines the survival value of psychic representation not only for an individual but also the human species as well (Beres, 1968; Compton, 1972).

Primary identification creates the foundation for two faculties in the advanced psychic organisation: on the one hand, it creates the frame for psychic representation; on the other it configures the future ego-ideal, in the frame of which drive satisfaction will be pursued without endangering one's primary narcissistic wellbeing and safety (Sandler, 1987). Conjointly with the superego, the ego-ideal comes to play a central role in affect regulation.

Only after the appropriate consolidation of the psychic structure in adolescence does moderate superego function become established. In consequence, the archaic law of Talion will be replaced by moderate principles of justice and the metaphorical interpretation of law. As it is a relatively recent psychic formation, the advanced superego forms a minor point of resistance in the psychic organisation which is prone to regression in the face of drive-instinctual dangers. When the capacity for psychic representation collapses in a traumatic situation, the conscience also tends to lose its metaphorical dimension. Then the crude id-impulses regain dominance within the superego with destructive consequences.

According to Leon Wurmser (1988, 1992, 1994) the importance of the superego has been neglected in psychoanalytic discussion to the extent that it is justified to speak of it as 'the sleeping giant' of psychoanalytic theory. This neglect applies especially to the psychoanalytic understanding of severe, non-psychotic conditions such as drug abuse, perversions, and narcissistic personality disorders. Wurmser's main point was that these clinical conditions derive from incongruent superego loyalties that are liable to provoke difficult shame-guilt dilemmas, resulting in the distortion of reality perception by withdrawing *affective validation* from what is perceived.

In the case of psychotic depression when the advanced superego function collapses, a *Verleugnung*, or disavowal of reality perceptions, may not be sufficient to pacify immoderate superego demands, but the affective experience as the carrier of painful meanings has to be destroyed. This takes place through a dissection of the link between original id ideas and the concomitant affect responses, corresponding to Bion's (1959) notion of 'attack on linking' and McDougall's (1989) observation of affect dispersal in psychosomatic disorders. In a schizophrenic fragmentation, the primal representative matrix becomes depleted of its vital drive-instinctual resources. Miss B's case can be located in the middle of these two pathological conditions.

My clinical vignette of President Anwar Sadat's assassination at the beginning of this chapter demonstrates dramatically how the recovery of a solid affect state may become possible when the lost connection between the drive-instinctual urge and the concomitant affect arousal becomes re-established. In Eric's case, the unconscious idea of patricide formed the key to understanding his short-lived recovery, but not the only one. Eric's ambivalence towards his inner mother and his oral aggression related to her also have to be taken into consideration. The main part of his aggression was directed towards himself as tyrannical superego demands. Surrendering to these demands, Eric felt completely unable to fulfil his mother's express wish that her son growing to become a decent man: that is, his ego-ideal. Eric's delusional belief that he had betrayed his mother's expectations resulted in pervasive feelings of shame and guilt. Witnessing President Sadat's murder on television furnished his preconscious ego with the idea of patricide, also opening the gates for experiencing the full affective intensity of his ambivalence towards his dead mother represented by his wife.

In a psychotic depression, the Oedipal guilt is dealt with by the ego resorting to early oral-cannibalistic phantasies and a fusion with the destroyed primary object, resulting in despair. Although this regression more often than not is rooted in the pre-Oedipal phase of psychic development, it cannot, however, be dealt with in the transference as if it were detached from intrapsychic conflict. It is important not to forget that dead *Jocasta* also belongs to the Oedipus myth.

Although many affects may exhibit a signal function, castration anxiety has a special role in this respect, which can be related to the fact that masturbation plays an important role in linking together bodily excitations and drive-instinctual ideation in adolescence (Laufer, 1989), serving to integrate affect experience consonant with one's sexual body and the genital reality. The final consolidation of superego structures coincides with this phase of psychosexual development.

Conclusion

At the crossroads outside Thebes Oedipus came to kill his father Laius, ostensibly without passion, literally in passing. Only retroactively did he come to understand the full affective meaning of his deed. The crime itself was a simple fact, representing the dismantled idea of the instinctual drive: patricide. Only after resolving the riddle of the Sphinx and recognising the son's sexual love for his mother was he able to face what had taken place. To avoid Jocasta's fate, i.e., desperation, Oedipus put out his eyes so that he did not see what he already knew to be true: his humiliation and guilt.

The psychoanalytic setting represents a metaphorical frame for an intrapsychic solution to the drive conflict. Within this frame, the disruptive experiences of the past can be dealt with without it necessarily signifying an overwhelming experience of shame and guilt. This integration is a major structural achievement enabling the recognition of reality without sacrificing vital affects and a genuine interest in life.

Note

1 The paper was originally published in *Scand. Psychoanal. Rev.*, 23: 50–64 (2000). Copyright© The Psychoanalytic Societies of Denmark, Finland, Norway, and Sweden, reprinted by permission of Taylor & Francis Ltd, www.tandfonline.com on behalf of The Psychoanalytic Societies of Denmark, Finland, Norway, and Sweden.

References

Beres, D. (1968). The humanness of human beings: Psychoanalytic considerations. *Psychoanal Q.*, 37: 487–522.

Bion, W. R. (1959). Attacks on linking. *Int. J. Psychoanal.*, 40: 308–315.

Compton, A. (1972). A study of the psychoanalytic theory of anxiety. II. Developments in the theory of anxiety since 1926. *J. Amer. Psychoanal. Assn.*, 20: 341–394.

Fenichel, O. (1946). *The Psychoanalytic Theory of Neurosis*. London: Routledge & Kegan Paul, Ltd.

Freud, S. (1915). Repression. In *The Standard Edition of the Complete Psychological Works of Sigmund Freud*, Volume XIV. London: The Hogarth Press and the Institute of Psychoanalysis, pp. 141–158.

Gaddini, E. (1982). Early defensive fantasies and the psychoanalytical process. *Int. J. Psychoanal.*, 63: 379–388.

Gaddini, E. (1992). *A Psychoanalytic Theory of Infantile Experience*. Limentani, A. (editor). London: Tavistock et Routledge.

Gaddini, R. and Gaddini, E. (1959). Rumination in infancy. In *Dynamic Psychopathology in Childhood*. Pavenstedt, E. and Jessner, L. (editors). New York: Grune and Stratton, pp. 166–185.

Green, A. (1977). Conceptions of affect. *Int. J. Psychoanal.*, 58: 129–156.

Green, A. (1986). The dead mother. In *On Private Madness*. London: The Hogarth Press and the Institute of Psychoanalysis, pp. 142–173. Reference to *Narcissisme vie: Narcissisme de mort*. Paris: Minuit, 1983.

Kernberg, O. (1984). *Severe Personality Disorders*. New Haven, CT and London: Yale University Press, p. 237.

Kernberg, O. (1994). Aggression, trauma, and hatred in the treatment of borderline patients. A paper read at the *Finnish Psychoanalytical Society*, 24 November.

Laplanche, J. (1976). *Life and Death in Psychoanalysis*. Baltimore, MD and London: The Johns Hopkins University Press.

Laufer, M. (1989). A body/mind continuum. *Psychoanal. Study Child*, 44: 281–294.

McDougall, J. (1985). *Theaters of the Mind*. New York: Basic Books, Inc.

McDougall, J. (1989). *Theaters of the Body: A Psychoanalytical Approach to Psychosomatic Illness*. New York and London: W. W. Norton.

Pao, P-N. (1979). *Schizophrenic Disorders*. New York: Int. Univ. Press.

Piha, H. (1985). Music in the speech: One way to the unconscious. A paper read at the *Finnish Psycho-Analytical Society*, May.

Piha, H. (2005). Intuition: A bridge to the coenesthetic world of experience. *J. Amer. Psychoanal. Assn.*, 53: 23–49.

Salonen, S. (1976). On the technique of the psychotherapy of schizophrenia. In *Schizophrenia 75*. Jörstad, J. and Ugelstad, E. (editors). Oslo: Universitetsforlag, pp. 115–133.

Sandler, J. (1987). *From Safety to Superego*. London: Karnac Books.

Sandler, J. and Rosenblatt, B. (1962). The concept of the representational world. *Psychoanal. Study Child*, 17: 128–145.

Schur, M. (1955). Comments on the metapsychology of somatization. *Psychoanal. Study Child*, 10: 119–164.

Schur, M. (1966). *The Id and the Regulatory Principles of Mental Functioning*. New York: Int. Univ. Press.

Searles, F. S. (1965). *Collected Papers on Schizophrenia and Related Subjects*. New York: Int. Universities Press.

Stein, R. (1999). *Psychoanalytic Theories of Affect*. London: Karnac Books.

Tähkä, V. (1993). *The Mind and Its Treatment*. Madison, CT, London: International Univ. Press.

Volkan, V. D. (1995). *The Infantile Psychotic Self and Its Fates*. Northvale, NJ, London: Jason Aronson Inc.

Wurmser, L. (1988). "The sleeping giant": A dissenting comment about borderline pathology. *Psychoanal. Inquiry*, 8: 373–397.

Wurmser, L. (1992). Psychology of compulsive drug use. In *The Chemically Dependent*. Walles, P. C. (editor). New York: Brunner/Matzel.

Wurmser, L. (1994). Zur Psychoanalyse schwerer psychischer Erkrankungen. *Forum Psychoanal.*, 10: 1–12.

7

UNDERSTANDING PSYCHOTIC DISORDER[1]

I referred previously to the Finnish verb *ymmärtää*, to understand. It derives from the noun *ympyrä*, the circle. To grasp the meaning of what is perceived, it has to become circumscribed in one's mind. If we don't understand something, we say that it transcends our comprehension or that it is beyond us. In other words, an object receives an inner meaning only after being located within a frame of reference. The clarity of scientific thinking requires a conceptual framework. Only scientists who accept the shared framework of their discipline and the requirements of their method are considered trustworthy. If this frame of reference becomes revoked, the possibilities of truthful discussion are also forfeited. In short, the integrity of the scientific community becomes lost. On the individual level, this situation is comparable to a psychotic condition, in which the capacity to deal with the drive-instinctual impulses within a shared human frame of reference has collapsed.

In a neurotic disorder, some aspects of reality perception are sacrificed for infantile wishful thinking. Then an individual behaves like the Japanese soldier who, according to a news item, had been hiding in the Indonesian jungle for many decades. He did not hear that World War II had ended until his capitulation to the local authorities. With the neurotic disorder the anachronistic intrapsychic conflict obstructs an individual's full capacity to feel sexual pleasure. The foundations of mutual understanding and the ability to deal with drive-instinctual impulses at the intrapsychic level have not been shattered.

However, we cannot approach a psychotic individual merely as a prisoner of anachronistic misinterpretation of genital reality, although this point also has to be considered carefully. Above all, he or she has lost the capacity to cope with perceptions and drive-instinctual impulses at the metaphorical level, which has far-reaching consequences both for psychic functioning and psychoanalytic treatment. In the light of Henrik Enckell's (2002) work, the psychotic patient does not have an integrated faculty of metaphor at his disposal, forming a prerequisite for the renewal of psychic experience in the transference.

To understand a psychotic state in more detail, we have to return to the emergence of the individual ego in the light of psychoanalytic knowledge. In studying the early identification phenomena, it has become possible to understand those psychic configurations within the frame of which the infant begins to outline his experiential world from within. In the case of psychotic individuals, the foundations of psychic experience have remained for some reason or another unstable and fragile, which then predisposes them to fall ill later in life. Regardless of the ultimate causes of the disorder, it is of primary importance to understand the particular vulnerability of the psychotic patient in each case (London, 1973).

According to Leo A. Spiegel (1959), the self creates a frame of reference for the individual's perceptual world and sense of identity. In taking Spiegel's work as his starting point, Heinz Lichtenstein (1961, 1964) maintained that the rudimentary core of individual identity derives from the early interaction between the infant and mother, as we have explored in depth in the preceding chapters. From the infant's viewpoint, this interaction is based on a phenomenon comparable to ethological imprinting in the animal world. However, to speak about imprinting in this connection may be misleading because the human infant is not endowed with the same inborn readiness as animal offspring (Beres, 1968). In any case, Lichtenstein maintained that the unique set of the mother's unconscious needs and wishes toward her child defines each child's individual identity. His concept of the *identity theme* refers to this phenomenon, which follows the individual throughout life as a kind of psychic organiser (Spitz, 1965).

I have studied the foundations of psychic experience from the viewpoint of extreme psychic trauma by taking Freud's notion of primary identification as my starting point. I first became interested in this topic while treating psychotic patients, who were incapable of dealing with their intrapsychic conflicts in the transference. On the other hand, I had observed how the normal psychic functioning of even the most fragmented schizophrenic patients could recover in a brief moment, as if they had awoken from a nightmare. In underscoring the theoretical importance of this observation, I would like to emphasise that the psychic integration thus attained is not necessarily lasting. A more permanent change requires arduous psychoanalytic work leading to a gradual differentiation and integration of the patient's inner world. Thus the therapeutic relationship with the psychotic patient should also serve the broad structuralisation of the patient's mind, according to Veikko Tähkä (1993).

The instant recovery of psychotic patients is analogous to an early phase of the child's psychic development. A panic convulsing the infant's entire person may abate in a brief moment when sensory contact with the primary object becomes restored. This phenomenon signifies the recovery of primary identification through which an internal frame of psychic experience becomes re-established in the infant's developing mind. According to Jean Laplanche (1976) this takes place originally when the infant finds another human being and at the same moment himself in the image of the other.

In the comedy *Heath Cobblers* by the Finnish writer Aleksis Kivi (1993), the principal character Esko comes close to the idea of primary identification. Prematurely rejoicing at his marriage to his sweetheart Kreeta, he contemplates the meaning of love as follows: 'Kreeta is Esko and Esko is Kreeta. In the metaphorical sense, this is true on the level of primary identification. The gradually evolving and differentiating experiential world will find a location within this configuration. In this mode, primary identification 'formats' the human mind to deal with inner meanings. But in a psychotic state, this formatting has collapsed.

After radical psychic trauma, the ego makes every endeavour to restore normal psychic functioning, or at least to prevent the disaster from escalating. Optimally, the recovery takes place without lasting damage; however, with a psychotic disorder the precarious psychic coherence can be maintained only by sacrificing a sense of reality and vital affects. The ultimate defence against the escalation of psychic trauma is resorting to a delusion which is no longer framed by primary identification but refers to autoerotic excitation and bizarre bodily sensations, forming a surrogate frame of reference for the individual's psychic survival. In this sense, the delusion serves as a substitutive identity theme, which also explains its great persistence during psychoanalytic treatment (Frosch, 1967). Analogical shortcuts of psychic functioning can also be observed in non-psychotic states, e.g., drug addictions, sexual perversions, and psychosomatic disorders.

Vamik D. Volkan (1997) has pointed out the ubiquitous occurrence of shared delusional frames at the group level. For example, an ethnic group that feels its identity collapsing may become easily agitated by grandiose ideological thought constructions, and hence susceptible to destructive deeds outside an individual's psychic representation. In facing the threat of annihilation, i.e. extreme psychic trauma, the members of the group may adhere to their paranoid leader's delusional frame of reference, possibly with disastrous consequences.

How do we approach a psychotic patient from the psychoanalytic point of view? In short, the therapeutic setting should, in the first place, represent the same human frame of reference that the parents originally brought to the child's id-perception, which the psychotic patient has fatefully lost by falling ill. This task may be possible if we are in genuine touch with the particular vulnerability of psychotic individuals. Perhaps the greatest value of our metapsychological models lies in providing the means for a definitive understanding of an individual's helplessness in this delicate territory of human vulnerability.

A clinical episode

I would still like to return to Beatrice's case described in the previous chapter. At the time of the incident to which I will now refer, one particular delusion had been puzzling us, consisting of the idea that a friend of hers was going to break into the house to damage her beautiful apartment, albeit not her. The precious tile stove was often felt to be the target of these evil intentions. Importantly, she lived alone in her childhood home after her parents' death.

Usually Beatrice was able to control her anxiety quite well without burdening her close relationships too much with her worries. Now and then, however, she felt so threatened that she was compelled to contact the police. In fact, Beatrice had become acquainted with a policeman who was able to listen to her with genuine sensitivity and understanding. Once, however, she met a higher-ranking officer who had the same surname as mine. After hearing Beatrice's story, he said: 'It would certainly be a fine idea if you contacted the other Salonen.'

In subsequently discussing this comic occurrence with her, we could both share the insight that her problem was not solvable by police intervention based on concrete evidence. Another frame of reference was necessary, within the confines of which her particular vulnerability could be dealt with on a metaphorical level.

Beatrice had found scratches on her tile stove, the existence of which I had no reason to doubt because time leaves its imprints everywhere. She had also found suspicious patches on the floor. In addition, she asked me for an explanation of how a paper clip could have got into her drug package. She surely had an explanation of her own, but how could she make me believe it? She began to despair because she had placed her trust in me. For my part, I felt helpless, and I could only reply that her conclusions were beyond me and that I was not able to think like her without losing my integrity. The atmosphere immediately changed, and she proceeded hopefully to say that one day she perhaps would also get the point. At that moment, I felt we were at the crux of my topic.

Many valuable psychoanalytic reconstructions had been attained in the course of her prolonged treatment. For example, it was evident that Beatrice had endeavoured to control the repercussions of her sexual trauma by resorting to the delusion, a trauma that had seriously disturbed the consolidation of her female self-image and left an excessive leakage in her affect regulation. A central task of our work was binding the flood of her overwhelming affect storm and rage into a meaningful context in the transference.

An additional analytic reconstruction concerned her home and its cherished furniture, representing for Beatrice the interior of her female body and her sexual wishes, perceived as an overwhelming threat to her psychic integrity. In displacing the most threatening drive-instinctual contents from the sphere of transference and metaphorical transformation to a delusional context, Beatrice aimed at safeguarding her precarious integrity from overwhelming excitation and rage, which so often had caused her psychic integrity to collapse. Although we met seldom during this phase, the sessions were of paramount importance for Beatrice in invigorating her primary identification. Within this frame, she was finally able to organise the course of her life meaningfully and find internal solutions to her intrapsychic conflict. Each of our meetings signified a small step towards psychic integration as well as a definitive understanding of her psychotic disorder as presented in the previous chapter.

Note

1 This paper was read at *the Yrjö O. Alanen Symposium*, Turku, February 2002, and published in *Scand. Psychoanal. Rev.*, 25: 143–146 (2002). Copyright©The Psychoanalytic Societies of Denmark, Finland, Norway and Sweden, reprinted by permission of Taylor & Francis Ltd, www.tandfonline.com on behalf of The Psychoanalytic Societies of Denmark, Finland, Norway, and Sweden.

References

Beres, D. (1968). The humanness of human beings: Psychoanalytic considerations. *Psychoanal Q.*, 37: 487–522.

Enckell, H. (2002). *Metaphor and the Psychodynamic Function of the Mind*. Kuopio: Kuopio University Publications D. Medical Sciences 265.

Frosch, J. (1967). Delusional fixity, sense of conviction, and the psychotic conflict. *Int. J Psychoanal.*, 48: 475–495.

Kivi, A. (1993). *Aleksis Kivi's Heath Cobblers (Nummisuutarit) and Kullervo Translated by Douglas Robinson*. St. Cloud, MI: North Star Press of St. Cloud.

Laplanche, J. (1976). *Life and Death in Psychoanalysis*. Baltimore, MD and London: The Johns Hopkins University Press.

Lichtenstein, H. (1961). Identity and sexuality – a study of their interrelationship in man. *J. Amer. Psychoanal. Assn.*, 9: 179–260.

Lichtenstein, H. (1964). The role of narcissism in the emergence and maintenance of a primary identity. *Int. J. Psychoanal.*, 45: 49–56.

London, N. J. (1973). An essay on psychoanalytic theory: Two theories of schizophrenia. Part I and II. *Int. J. Psychoanal.*, 54: 169–193.

Spiegel, L. A. (1959). The self, the sense of self, and perception. *Psychoanal. Study Child*, 14: 81–109.

Spitz, R. (1965). *The First Year of Life*. New York: Int. Univ. Press.

Tähkä, V. (1993). *Mind and Its Treatment: A Psychoanalytical Approach*. Madison, CT: Int. Univ. Press.

Volkan, V. D. (1997). *Blood Lines: From Ethnic Pride to Ethnic Terrorism*. New York: Farrar, Straus and Giroux.

8

THE VULNERABLE CORE
The unconscious wish reconsidered[1]

Having chosen the unconscious as our theme, I would like to consider our starting points carefully, lest we imagine that through our method we have been able to tame the elemental psychic forces discovered by psychoanalysis. Leo Rangell (1974) compared the psychoanalytic interpretation to a flashlight pointing into the Grand Canyon. We glimpse in one shot only a small area of the magnificent landscape, then it fades into the darkness of repression. Nor can we capture the unconscious with theoretical abstractions, which are tools by which we discuss and think about this part of human reality and are useful only as far as they serve to deepen psychoanalytic understanding. They constitute the conceptual space within which our observations acquire shared meanings.

Someone who has been living in a foreign culture and then returns home may be anxious about being unable to convey his experience to those who cannot share his frame of reference. Freud understood that the dream offers a common frame of reference in attempting to approach the unconscious psychic reality. The same also applies to myths. In the course of time, the psychoanalytic experience itself has become a common point of reference. We find ourselves in the fortunate position of being able to refer to the vast clinical experience documented by previous generations of analysts. However, we are still in the same situation as our predecessors. How can we convey to our fellow analysts the moments of insight that are already fading from our conscious minds like dreams? There is a long distance to travel from our preliminary observations to the point of documenting them as psychoanalytic discoveries. Like latent dreams, analytic knowledge ultimately concerns unconscious wishes constituting the hidden core of the human mind.

Moving from the first, topographic theory of psychic functioning to the structural theory has deeply affected our understanding of unconscious psychic processes. However, the new perspectives, including a spatial shaping of psychic reality, have not diminished the importance of the topographic point of view. On the contrary, they have deepened it. Anna Freud addressed this point in recommending her own 'bad habit' of living between these two frames of reference because this greatly facilitates psychoanalytic thinking (Sandler and A. Freud, 1985, pp. 32–33).

The concept of the unconscious as the starting point underlines our common theoretical origins. Freud's structural view already divides the psychoanalytic community, notwithstanding his dualistic theory of the instinctual drives – that is, the life drive and death drive. Against this background, I will consider the *unconscious wish* and its importance for analysts today. Not only is the vulnerability of human beings related to it, but also vital affects and primary narcissistic interest in life.

The wish, the fantasy, and the wishful fantasy

Joseph Sandler approached the problem of the unconscious by placing emphasis on Freud's topographic formulations. Sandler's analysis of the preconscious is particularly useful. Although being descriptively unconscious, the preconscious does not function according to the primary process but follows the logic of waking life, corresponding to the unconscious ego of Freud's structural model. While the Kleinian school approaches psychic contents from the viewpoint of early oral-introjective phantasy, Sandler, by contrast, visualised interaction between fantasies and wishes on different levels of psychic functioning. Only after reaching the preconscious is the psychic content capable of becoming conscious in the analytic relationship. On the other hand, the preconscious as well as conscious fantasies may return to the id as a result of repression, where they will be treated like original memory traces, forming a genuine part of the primitive psychic process as the ideational contents of drive-instinctual wishes (Sandler and Nagera, 1963). Wishful fantasies and unconscious wishes thus become intertwined to form a psychic matrix constituting the entire representational world. According to Sandler (1976), instinctual wishes are a fundamental psychic category and not fantasy: 'Essentially the unconscious is an organised, disguised, unconscious modification and elaboration of an unsatisfied wish.'

Joseph Sandler and Anne-Marie Sandler (1994, 1998) aimed to bring psychoanalytic theory closer to clinical experience. Their notion of the present and past unconscious, in particular, facilitates this purpose by referring the former to the unconscious ego and the latter to the early origins of psychic development – that is, to the child's unconscious. The present unconscious can be retrieved through immediate interaction in the analytical relationship. By contrast, the past unconscious can be reached only through psychoanalytic interpretation and reconstruction. Joseph Sandler's (1989) essay 'The id – or the child within?' exemplifies his aim.

The Kleinian theory places psychoanalytic thinking in the area of the early oral-introjective interaction between the infant and mother. Oedipal themes are also viewed from this perspective, which signifies a radical change from Freud's theory of the Oedipus complex as a principal organiser (Etchegoyen, 1985). The early fantasies linked to the breast and the mother's body are seen as the nodal point of psychoanalytic thinking (Isaacs, 1948). Early psychic development is then visualised from the viewpoint of psychic survival, with the infant's early agonies being dealt with in terms of splitting, denial, and projective identification in the transference. What is at stake here is the helpless ego dealing with vital affects of love and hate, reflecting the struggle between the life and the death instincts in the unconscious. The solution to this conflict can be achieved with a new level of psychic integration: the depressive position.

According to Ruth Stein (1999), Klein's comprehensive notion of the schizo-paranoid and depressive positions represents a large-scale, dual model of anxiety and guilt. In this respect, Klein's theory is comparable to Freud's later theory of anxiety. In Freud's structural model final integration is achieved through the major identifications and internalisations as a result of the resolution of the Oedipus complex. The ego then acquires the capacity for governing unconscious psychic processes at the level of a new autonomy (Freud, 1926). However different, it is important to keep these two conceptualizations in mind in our efforts to understand the unconscious wish within the overall psychic organisation.

The wish as a functional unit

The Finnish noun *mieliteko*, 'desire', opens a window onto our topic. It denotes an act carried out in mind. If a drive-instinctual impulse is unable to achieve its aim in the external world, it becomes represented as an equivalent act on the intrapsychic level, linked with the memory trace of the previous satisfaction, thus forming a functional unit indicating the unconscious wish. The evolving human mind consists of a matrix of these wishes. The focus of psychoanalytic interest is this realm, from its elementary shapes to the major psychic configurations that unfold before our eyes during psychoanalytic treatment.

In his monograph *The Id and the Regulatory Principles of Mental Functioning* (1966), Max Schur approaches the unconscious wish from the structural point of view. By taking Freud's notion of *perceptual identity* (1900, p. 566) as his starting point, Schur links a rudimentary ego aspect even to the elementary wishes aimed at discharging of drive-instinctual tensions within the id. Aren't these wishes also based on perceptions and memory traces reactivated when necessary? As a matter of fact, Schur visualises the unconscious wish as a *functional unit in the id*. By becoming interwoven into psychic functioning on all levels of psychic development, the wishes will then constitute the unconscious psychic reality from within, as it were. In Schur's opinion, the id, the ego, and the superego are not demarcated from each other very clearly, but they form a functional continuity. The id therefore evolves not only phylogenetically, but ontogenetically as well, which is consonant with Joseph Sandler's view mentioned above.

The continuity of the psychic faculties also helps us understand Freud's notion of id-perception in *An Outline of Psycho-Analysis* (1940):

> The id, cut off from the external world, has a world of perception of its own. It detects with extraordinary acuteness certain changes in its interior, especially oscillations in the tension of its instinctual needs, and these changes become conscious as feelings in the pleasure-unpleasure series. It is hard to say, to be sure, by what means and with the help of what sensory terminal organs these perceptions come about. But it is an established fact that self-perceptions – coenesthetic feelings of pleasure and unpleasure – govern the passage of events in the id with despotic force.
>
> (p. 198)

In fact, the perceptive-sensory dimension of the human mind is of great importance when thinking about these elementary drive phenomena in more detail. The issue is not only the sensations of the pleasure-unpleasure series in the unconscious but also the perceptions and the affect responses related to the ideational contents of instinctual drives. From the viewpoint of the rudimentary ego, these contents appear as actual deeds (Baranger et al., 1988). Do they manifest an innate inclination to instinct – driven deeds, according to Freud, – or are they derived from the infant's seduction by the early human environment, as Laplanche (1997) proposes? Green (2000) seems to endorse Freud's position. In any case, these elementary phenomena prevailing in the id determine the child's future development as well as the parents' unconscious attitudes towards their children. Before these archaic id-elements occur as wishes, they have to find a human frame of reference, which leads us to primary identification.

The wish for primary identification

According to Daniel Widlöcher (1985), the wish for identification with the object and the wish to have a relationship with it represent a fundamental dualism in Freud's thinking, which has been hidden behind another dualism, namely the life and death instincts. Widlöcher thinks that many conceptual misunderstandings could have been avoided if we had only been able to see that identification has an instinctual origin of its own, instead of linking it to the oral-incorporative urge to have the object. Particularly, Freud's (1923, p. 31) notion of primary identification has been difficult to understand, because it does not presuppose an existing object tie. According to Freud, it takes place before object libidinal cathexes. In the light of Widlöcher's analysis, this becomes more understandable, as primary identification has an instinctual origin of its own as a mode of object finding.

From these starting points, we can understand more clearly the revolutionary impact primary identification has on the development of the human mind. It is primary identification which creates the fundamental conditions for dealing with elementary drive phenomena on the level of a wish, as well as heralding the beginnings of the psychic organisation.

The ego-ideal is customarily seen as a derivative of primary narcissism and the infant's maternal fusion (Hoffer, 1952; Jacobson, 1965; Chasseguet-Smirgel, 1985). It is thought to represent a lost paradise projected onto the future, which vitalises psychic experience and anticipation of future satisfaction. An unparalleled psychic intensity is linked with it, which an individual seeks throughout life, without ever fully attaining it. There is no direct access to this blissful state of mind without violating one's psychic integrity. It remains beyond primal repression. Therefore, it can be approached only metaphorically.

My clinical experience supports Freud's view that primary identification is a direct and immediate perceptual phenomenon taking place before ordinary object ties. When the infant first finds the object, the corresponding configuration becomes established within its emerging mind as a metaphor. This configuration will form a frame of reference for the psychic representation. As projected onto the future, it outlines a state of well-being and integrity: the ego-ideal. As a vulnerable psychic configuration, the ego-ideal may collapse later in life with destructive consequences. On the other hand, the wish for psychic survival also becomes linked to this configuration.

Repetition compulsion is not only a destructive phenomenon, but it also serves to restore primary identification (Lichtenstein, 1964; Caldwell, 1976). If this fails, as so often is the case, the helpless ego will resort to oral destructive fantasies and projective-introjective defences to restore normal psychic functioning, or to 'fantasies in the body' (Gaddini, 1982) on the psychosomatic front. A recovery of primary identification in the transference may in this situation form a turning point in psychoanalytic treatment.

Ms D's early agonies

As a child, Ms D had repeatedly been treated in a distant hospital for a psychosomatic condition, for the first time at the age of one year and two months, then at the age of five. After many years of psychoanalytic work, we could reconstruct the little girl's agonising state of despair related to her separation from home, encapsulated in her mind for decades, and her secrete wish for the recovery of her primary identification. The analytic session concerned proceeded as follows:

> Last time I was completely reluctant to consider my mother's death. Then, at the end of the session, something peculiar happened, after your having said that being frustrated is no sin. I felt myself being definitively alone, without any people around. Pain and desolation

belong to this state of mind. The Good Samaritan occurs to me, but what differs is that in this parable there were still other people around. The robbery still occurred. My experience was like listening to distant traffic noise, without any sense affect. There was no time. It must relate to a very early experience. There was no hope, but I was not hopeless either. Being hopeless is already feeling. There was no blaming there. It feels strange, but I do not accuse my mother anymore. Being in this state is nobody's fault. One only gets into it.

(Salonen, 1997, p. 63)

In another context, we had met in town by chance. Ms D told me that this had been a shocking experience for her because she felt that I had perceived hidden love in her glance. She had always avoided eye contact with me. The next session took then a dramatic course. In the beginning, she said warmly (p. 66):

"If someone touches me, I am like molten wax" Then her voice became ice-cold, and she continued in a hostile tone: "By the way, do you remember the film *Touch of Evil*? You know the bad guys earn their lot. . . . This is to disparage what I told you yesterday about my love. It's a matter of indifference now because you will never touch me. . . . If only someone evil would do it, at least – pain. The murderer occurs to me. I can't live without somebody touching me."

The Finnish word *koskea*, touch, also signifies feeling pain. We understood that her sufferings were related to the little girl's wish for gentle bodily intimacy with her parents after having been left in the hospital. Ms D's psychoanalytic process had reached not only the source of her cold narcissism, but also her vulnerable wish for sensorial intimacy with her parents, and for the recovery of her primary identification.

Subsequently her Oedipal wishes were dealt with in transference. Being sent to hospital at the age of five had signified for her a banishment for her hidden sexual wishes. As the analysis came to a conclusion, it was clear that the core of Ms D's intrapsychic conflict consisted of the wrathful Oedipal father turning his face away from his daughter, thus signifying her love was worthless. The little girl's agonising despair had finally been bound into an intrapsychic conflict that it was possible to resolve in transference.

The analyst cannot compensate for the analysand's misfortunes in life. Instead, he or she should maintain the psychoanalytic setting where the analysand's genuine wish for primary identification may be reconstructed in the transference. If successful, this reconstruction signifies a crucial step from traumatic helplessness toward normal psychic functioning and resolving the intrapsychic conflict.

The viewpoint of structural conflict

As a result of being linked with an object at different levels of psychic development, unconscious wishes constitute a psychic reality from within. In becoming progressively differentiated, these wishes decisively contribute both to the inner experiential world and psychic functioning leading to individuation and autonomy (Tähkä, 1993).

I have stressed the importance of primary identification because it configures the early frame of reference for dealing with elementary drive phenomena at the wish level. Psychic integrity is based on this configuration. As projected into the future, it constitutes the ego-ideal within the frame of which the archaic superego demands can ultimately find a metaphorical interpretation. In this way, the advanced superego becomes consolidated, stabilising psychic regulation consonant with the realities of life. This achievement touches upon what Leo Rangell (1967, 1990) called *the human core* in referring to the intrapsychic conflict and its solution in psychoanalysis.

Libidinal wishes become associated in the unconscious with the drive-instinctual dangers of separation, castration, and the loss of love. While the child is still unable to understand these threats at a metaphorical level, he or she will conceive of them concretely. The most delicate task of the psychoanalytic endeavour is to reach the Oedipal wishes. To understand that these wishes and the drive-instinctual dangers associated with them are id-elements from the past, i.e. 'the child within', makes it possible to understand that loss and vulnerability are an integral part of human life. A new temporal perspective will then be constituted in the experiential world, indicating a structural integration of psychic functioning.

Conclusion

I have been analysing the wish as a functional unit of unconscious psychic processes. As a result of being linked with objects at different levels of psychic development, the unconscious wish constitutes psychic reality. However, this is not possible without primary identification first creating the preconditions for dealing with elementary drive phenomena at the level of wish. This configuration is vulnerable and may collapse, with fatal consequences. If the unconscious wish as the carrier of normal psychic functioning fails, the ego is faced with radical psychic trauma. In representing the principle of primary identification, the psychoanalytic setting creates prerequisites for the recovery of normal psychic functioning at the elementary level of the unconscious wish.

Note

1 The paper was originally read at the *EPF Annual Conference*, Helsinki, April 2004.

References

Baranger, M., Baranger, W. and Mom, J. M. (1988). The infantile psychic trauma from us to Freud: pure trauma, retroactivity and reconstruction. *Int. J. Psychoanal.*, 69: 113–128.

Caldwell, R. S. (1976). Primal identity. *Int. Rev. Psychoanal.*, 3: 417–433.

Chasseguet-Smirgel, J. (1985). *The Ego Ideal*. London: Free Association Books.

Etchegoyen, R. H. (1985). Identification and its vicissitudes. *Int. J. Psychoanal.*, 66: 3–18.

Freud, S. (1900). The interpretation of dreams. In *The Standard Edition of the Complete Psychological Works of Sigmund Freud*, Volume IV. London: The Hogarth Press and the Institute of Psychoanalysis, pp. 550–572.

Freud, S. (1923). The ego and the id. In *The Standard Edition of the Complete Psychological Works of Sigmund Freud*, Volume XIX. London: The Hogarth Press and the Institute of Psychoanalysis, pp. 1–66.

Freud, S. (1926). Inhibitions, symptoms and anxiety. In *The Standard Edition of the Complete Psychological Works of Sigmund Freud*, Volume XX. London: The Hogarth Press and the Institute of Psychoanalysis, pp. 75–176.

Freud, S. (1940). An outline of psycho-analysis. In *The Standard Edition of the Complete Psychological Works of Sigmund Freud*, Volume XXIII. London: The Hogarth Press and the Institute of Psychoanalysis, pp. 139–208.

Gaddini, E. (1982). Early defensive fantasies and the psychoanalytical process. *Int. J. Psychoanal.*, 63: 379–388.

Green, A. (2000). *Chains of Eros: The Sexual in Psychoanalysis*. London: Rebus Press.

Hoffer, W. (1952). The mutual influences in the development of ego and id: Earliest stages. *Psychoanal. Study Child*, 7: 31–41.

Isaacs, S. (1948). The nature and function of phantasy. *Int. J. Psychoanal.*, 29: 73–97.

Jacobson, E. (1965). *The Self and the Object World*. London: Hogarth Press.

Laplanche, J. (1997). The theory of seduction and the problem of the other. *Int. J. Psychoanal.*, 78: 653–666.

Lichtenstein, H. (1964). The role of narcissism in the emergence and maintenance of a primary identity. *Int. J. Psychoanal.*, 45: 49–56.

Rangell, L. (1967). Psychoanalysis, affects, and the 'human core'. On the relationship of psychoanalysis to the behavioural sciences. *Psychoanal. Q.*, 36: 172–202.

Rangell, L. (1974). A psychoanalytic perspective leading currently to the syndrome of the compromise of integrity. *Int. J. Psychoanal.*, 55: 3–12.

Rangell, L. (1990). *The Human Core: The Intrapsychic Base of Behavior*, Volume 1. Madison, CT: International Universities Press, pp. 353–468.

Salonen, S. (1997). Humiliation and dignity: Reflections on ego integrity. In *Seed of Madness: Constitution, Environment, and Fantasy in the Organization of the Psychotic Core*. Volkan, V. D. and Akhtar, S. (editors). Madison, CT: Int. Univ. Press, pp. 59–79.

Sandler, J. (1976). Dreams, unconscious fantasies and 'identity of perception'. *Int. R. Psychoanal.*, 3: 33–42.

Sandler, J. (1989). The id – or the child within? In *Dimensions of Psychoanalysis*. Sandler, J. (editor). London: Karnac Books.

Sandler, J. and Freud, A. (1985). *The Analysis of Defence: The Ego and the Mechanisms of Defence Revisited*. New York: Int. Univ. Press.

Sandler, J. and Nagera, H. (1963). Aspects of the metapsychology of fantasy. *Psychoanal. Study Child*, 18: 159–194.

Sandler, J. and Sandler, A.-M. (1994). Phantasy and its transformations: A contemporary Freudian view. *Int. J. Psych -Anal.*, 75: 387–394.

Sandler, J. and Sandler, A.-M. (1998). *Internal Objects Revisited*. London: Karnac Books.

Schur, M. (1966). *The Id and the Regulatory Principles of Mental Functioning*. New York: Int. Univ. Press.

Stein, R. (1999). *Psychoanalytic Theories of Affect*. London: Karnac Books.

Tähkä, V. (1993). *Mind and Its Treatment: A Psychoanalytical Approach*. Madison, CT: Int. Univ. Press.

Widlöcher, D. (1985). The wish for identification and structural effects in the work of Freud. *Int. J. Psychoanal.*, 66: 31–46.

9

ON DESTRUCTIVE DRIVE PHENOMENA
A study of human aggression[1]

In this chapter, I will comment on Freud's later dualistic drive theory in the light of Ms O's case history, in which destructive drive phenomena led to fatal consequences. I also intend to provide a framework for understanding the feelings of ambivalence and confusion that Freud's (1920) *Beyond the Pleasure Principle* may evoke in the reader. Despite its controversial reception, this work signified a turning point in the history of psychoanalytic thought.

Previously, it had been presumed that the aims of pursuing pleasure and avoiding unpleasure regulated unconscious psychic processes. Destructive drive phenomena were considered to be subject to the regime of this regulation, manifesting the sexual or self-preservative drives. The transition in Freud's thinking is often linked to his life history and the destruction unleashed by World War I. The shattering of personal object ties and narcissistic ideals both at the individual and public level could partly explain why the founder of psychoanalysis was compelled to embark on the search for a new theoretical synthesis only a few years after he had established a substantial and commonly shared theoretical foundation for his subject. Ten years later, Freud described this period of transition in a personal tone as follows:

> Starting from speculations on the beginning of life and from biological parallels, I drew the conclusion that, besides the instinct to preserve living substance and to join it into ever larger units, there must exist another, contrary instinct seeking to dissolve those units

and to bring them back to their primeval, inorganic state. That is to say, as well as Eros there was an instinct of death. The phenomena of life could be explained from the concurrent or mutually opposing action of these two instincts. It was not easy, however, to demonstrate the activities of this supposed death instinct. The manifestations of Eros were conspicuous and noisy enough. It might be assumed that the death instinct operated silently within the organism towards its dissolution, but that, of course, was no proof. A more fruitful idea was that a proportion of the instinct is diverted towards the external world and comes to light as an instinct of aggressiveness and destructiveness.

(1930, pp. 118–119)

Freud then proceeded:

The assumption of the existence of an instinct of death or destruction has met with resistance even in analytic circles; I am aware that there is a frequent inclination rather to ascribe whatever is dangerous and hostile in love to an original bipolarity in its own nature. To begin with it was only tentatively that I put forward the views I have developed here, but in the course of time they have gained such a hold upon me that I can no longer think in any other way.

(Ibid.) [Notes omitted]

In *Freud: Living and Dying*, Max Schur (1972) analyses the concept of the death instinct in light of Freud's life history and relates it to his ambivalence in facing his death. This argument is based not only upon biographical facts but also on Schur's relationship with Freud, as he was his personal physician until the death of his patient. Freud's ambivalence manifested not only in his neurotic symptoms but also in his tendency towards occult thinking – according to Schur. Freud's dilemma, as he aged, was how to meet the finiteness of life without resorting to metaphysical speculations outside of psychoanalysis, which may explain why there is an element of personal conviction or belief in his radical proposal of the dual drives:

Therefore, the formulation of the death-instinct concept – paradoxical as this may seem, may not only have steeled Freud for the 16-year ordeal of his cancer but prepared him for his belief in the supremacy of the ego, of the intellect, of *Logos*, the only force with which he could face *Ananke*. It paved the way for the Future of an illusion and for the formulation of a 'scientific Weltanschauung'.

(Schur, 1972, p. 332)

The divided followers

Many psychoanalysts belonging to Freud's proximate circle adopted the concept of the death drive, including Paul Federn (1956), who applied it to the treatment of psychotic conditions and narcissistic disorders in an original way, presaging present-day self-psychology. However, he differed with Freud in postulating a particular quality of psychic energy (*mortido*) for the death drive. Just as the libido becomes satisfied in the form of sexual pleasure, so does the mortido find its satisfaction in pain: *Schmerz*.

Melanie Klein (1948) belongs to those analysts who adopted Freud's dualistic drive theory as a foundation for her psychoanalytic thinking. Her starting point was the primitive anxieties and the threat of annihilation, which she directly linked with the influence of the death drive in the infant's mind. While the struggle between life and death continues throughout life, the death drive forms the ultimate source not only of primitive anxieties but all subsequent anxieties. According to Ruth Stein (1991), Klein created a new theory of anxiety not based on Freud's metapsychology. She took the primitive affect states of love and hate as her starting point. Envy is the most important explanatory factor of destructive drive phenomena, the psychic integration of which forms the crux of psychoanalytic therapy. This integration takes place initially on the part-object level in terms of projective and introjective identification, and subsequently in relation to the whole object when psychic regulation has been transferred from the schizo-paranoid position to the depressive position, thus creating the prerequisite for coping with the agonising threat of annihilation without resorting to a splitting of the object- and self-experience.

Although many of Freud's colleagues, including Klein, adopted the theory of the death drive without ambivalence, and applied it explicitly in their technique, the mainstream of psychoanalysis remained more reserved and left its possible verification to future biological research. Instead, the interest of the mainstream focused on the drive character of aggression, many seeing it as an independent instinctual drive and others linking it traditionally to the sexual drive and the vicissitudes of narcissism. In any case, Freud's structural insights, above all the conceptualisation of the superego, opened up radically new perspectives for understanding destructive drive phenomena, even without recourse to the notion of the death drive (Loewenstein, 1957; Fenichel, 1945).

The International Psychoanalytical Congress held in Vienna in 1971 formed an important stage in this discussion. Above all, Anna Freud's contribution at this Congress clarified our problem:

> It was never implied in Freud's dualistic biological theory that the life drive is the actual source of the sexual urges; the latter was always acknowledged as being either hormonal or anatomical. Nor need the death drive be the actual source of aggression. Clinically speaking, both have their own material sources, known or unknown, while simultaneously being what might be called the "representatives on earth" of the two supra-ordinated biological forces with opposite goals, the presence of which they presuppose. We may say equally, with regard to "aim", that clinically speaking, i.e., on earth, both libido and aggression pursue their own limited and mundane aims, while serving at the same time, the vaster biological purposes of life and death.
>
> (Freud, A., 1972, p. 171)

Although no consensus was attained in Vienna on the nature of destructive drive phenomena, and many participants were sceptical about whether any progress had been made in this area after Freud, the achievements of this Congress were nevertheless substantial. In addition to Anna Freud's presentation, the papers given by Kurt Eissler and Herbert Rosenfeld, both of which dealt with pathological narcissism, as well as Eugenio Gaddini's paper (1972) on the administration of aggression in the infant's early somato-psychic person, were original contributions.

Eissler's (1971) 'Death drive, ambivalence, and narcissism' dealt with destructive drive phenomena from both individual and societal viewpoints, posing the question of why human aggression dramatically exceeds what is necessary for self-preservation. Eissler came to the conclusion that the interplay of aggression, narcissism, and individual ambivalence may lead to disastrous consequences. Eissler believed that even the most advanced achievements of civilisation and individual psychic development cannot safeguard society against human destructiveness:

> The accomplishments produced by the formation of ego structure – for example, the ego's ability to neutralize aggression to the extent where non-defensive ego activities are also able to evolve – all these should not prevent us from perceiving that, despite such achievements of taming aggression and of placing it in the service of the greatest accomplishments, man still continues to participate, by commission or omission, in the gratification of the grossest sort of aggression and destruction. By means of a fine web of denial, he blots out those feelings of guilt that would be only too commensurate with the misdeeds in which he has had a hand, either directly or indirectly, and in that way, he gratifies in full measure his aggressive heritage which his ambivalence and narcissistic self-aggrandizement demand.
> (1971, pp. 69-70)

Rosenfeld (1971) related destructive drive phenomena to pathological islands of narcissism that are difficult to identify in the therapeutic relationship because they have been dissociated from the main part of psychic experience and are therefore silent. These islands do not represent a de-fusion of drives, according to Freud, but on the contrary, a pathological fusion in which a particular amalgam of narcissistic libido and aggression tends to multiply the power of aggression, which should otherwise decrease. Rosenfeld differentiated between normal libidinal narcissism, based on the idealisation of a good object, and pathological narcissism, based on the idealisation of omnipotent destructiveness and death, the ultimate objective being the denial of genuine libidinal dependence on another human being. The most stubborn forms of defence, including the negative therapeutic reaction, receive their destructive power from this kind of pathological narcissism. The primary task of the psychoanalytic treatment of these patients is to integrate their genuine libidinal dependence, which becomes possible only after first reaching these islands of pathological narcissism at the level of infantile experience:

> In terms of the infantile situation, the narcissistic patient wants to believe that he has given life to himself and is able to feed and look after himself. When he is faced with the reality of being dependent on the analyst, standing for the parents, particularly the mother,

he would prefer to die, to be non-existent, to deny the fact of his birth, and also to destroy his analytic progress and insight representing the child in himself, which he feels the analyst, representing the parents, has created. Frequently, at this point, the patient wants to give up the analysis but more often he acts out in a self-destructive way by spoiling his professional success and his personal relations. Some of these patients become suicidal and the desire to die, to disappear into oblivion, is expressed quite openly and death is idealized as a solution to all problems.

(Rosenfeld, 1971, p. 173)

Epistemological ambiguity in psychoanalytic theory

The multidimensional nature of Freud's *Beyond the Pleasure Principle* (1920) gives rise to substantial difficulties for those who sincerely accept its intellectual challenge, a challenge that has led to diverse interpretations of this work. Pentti Ikonen and Eero Rechardt (1978, 1993) approached Freud from a hermeneutic point of view, perceiving psychoanalysis as a science that does not aim at causal explanations of phenomena, like the natural sciences, but approaches the human mind through the interpretation of unconscious meanings. Respectively, the authors see Freud's reflections on biology merely as an expression of his natural philosophy, serving as the temporary scaffolding for his purely psychological theory until it was completed. After an extensive theoretical and epistemological discussion, the authors arrive at their interpretation of Freud's dual drives. According to these authors, the action of the life drive and the death drive underlie all psychic phenomena. By persistently reaching for new vital connections, *Eros* evokes restlessness in life, whereas *Thanatos* aims at binding this restlessness, its ultimate objective being an experiential state of peace. According to this interpretation, destructive drive phenomena are seen as abortive attempts at peace or perversions of *Thanatos*. Ikonen and Rechardt demonstrate this point of view by applying it to many clinical situations and phenomena, the psychoanalytic understanding of which would otherwise be a much more arduous task. This relatively easy application of Freud's concepts raises the question of whether something essential belonging to the sphere of psychoanalytic interest might, however, remain outside their scope. I am inclined to think that while the purely hermeneutic approach may apply to the area of healthy psychic functioning, it is not in the same way relevant to those areas where psychic representation of the elementary drive phenomena has failed or been traumatically shattered.

Freud (1924) never renounced the biological foundation of his drive theory. On the contrary, he held out hope that future biological research would some day cast additional light on this problem, which he considered the most enigmatic part of psychoanalytic theory. Psychoanalysis is located in an intermediate zone between a positivist and a hermeneutic approach without identifying itself entirely with either of them (Torsti-Hagman, 2003). This can be explained by the fact that the human mind is constituted from two different sources. Through the corporeal and genetic dispositions, it is linked to physical reality, which inevitably embodies the principle of natural causality and individual mortality. Through primary identification, the human mind has been furnished with the capability of dealing with the causal necessities of life on a metaphorical level. In having a bodily source, the instinctual drive is simultaneously open to inner meanings at the metaphorical level (Laplanche, 1976; Enckell, 2002). The Janus-faced quality of Freud's theory, culminating in the concept of the instinctual drive, creates an intellectual atmosphere out of which psychoanalytic inquiry emerges. According to Leo Rangell (1967), the subject of psychoanalysis as a science is *human nature*.

Scientific creativity in the service of psychic survival

According to Lis Lind (1991), Freud was confronted with many incongruous challenges in his search for a new synthesis of psychoanalytic theory. The first challenge was repetition compulsion, which did not necessarily require the notion of the death drive for its explanation. Repetition compulsion could also have been explained as a general characteristic of the instinctual drives. The second was the integration of aggression and destructive drive phenomena within the framework of psychoanalytic theory. In this respect, the notion of the death drive has proved to be highly evocative in binding together these phenomena, so that almost every psychoanalyst can intuitively follow a theoretical discussion of this topic. Freud's third problem, according to Lind, was related to his personal convictions and beliefs i.e. his *Weltanschauung*. At this point, Freud arrived at a surprising and apparently contradictory conclusion. According to him, repetition compulsion represents the conservative tendency of drives to return to the starting point of organic life. Paradoxically, not only the death drive but also the life drive ultimately pursues this same objective: the individual's death. Thus, Freud came to conceive of death as casting an ever-present shadow on human life in terms of his new drive theory.

Through psychoanalytic experience, we know how creativity may ensure individual psychic survival. In referring to a child's primal scene, we may ask whether the impetus for scientific thinking also emerges from a preconscious wish to transcend the threatening divide between perceived reality and the individual's capacity to comprehend it. I would like to think that amid his scientific ambitions, Freud was also dealing by means of creative thinking with his early psychic trauma – that is, the death of his brother Julius – to integrate it into the sphere of psychoanalytic understanding. At the utmost borders of psychic experience, such an integrative task required exceptional courage and an even more risky hypothesis.

In *Repression*, Freud (1915) had dealt with the drive-instinctual foundations of psychic experience, maintaining that the first representative of the instinctual drive would never become conscious as such, but will remain concealed beyond primal repression, thus preserving the enigma of the emergent human mind. However, in *Beyond the Pleasure Principle* (1920), Freud returned to this problem, approaching it from the viewpoint of psychic trauma. He proposed that instinctual drives ultimately exhibit a fundamental opposition between the forces of life and death. To cope with this polarity, the individual is compelled to search for inner solutions on new levels of psychic organisation. To succeed in this integrative task signifies psychic survival, which forms the counterpoint to traumatic helplessness and despair.

Against this background, the task of psychoanalytic treatment is to reconstruct an individual's traumatic helplessness in the context of unconscious wishes and drive-instinctual dangers of separation, castration, and the loss of love. This is possible only after the recovery of primary identification in the psychoanalytic setting. A more permanent integration of destructive drive phenomena and human aggression takes place on the genital level of psychic organisation, which means the awareness of possessing and using capabilities not only for acts of love but also for acts of destruction.

The fate of Ms O

Ms O's treatment took place in a hospital over a period of three years at a frequency of three times a week. When we met for the first time,

Ms O's condition was characterised by her fanatic hostility towards her mother as well as by serious suicidal ideation and autistic withdrawal. Her somatic condition was alarming because she had stopped taking care of vital physiological needs. It was not only her apparent lack of inner aliveness that was conspicuous, but her personality also evoked in me the impression of internal destruction infiltrating her entire person. At the same time, another aspect was also perceptible, namely a fragile attachment to me, which then formed a sustaining, albeit insufficient constituent of the therapeutic relationship.

Preceding her falling ill six years earlier, Ms O had experienced a profound narcissistic insult in her work as a creative artist resulting in the collapse of her ego-ideal. First, she became overwhelmed by horror, which soon gave way to mystical excitation. Seized by erotic hallucinations, she broke off her engagement and became absorbed for years in delusions. She told me she had believed, like Jean d'Arc, that she was a male, sometimes Napoleon, Nietzsche, or even Field Marshal Mannerheim's horse returning from war, wounded in the leg. However, at times she could understand that her delusions represented a defence against her feelings of great helplessness. Most of all, she experienced herself as living in a desolate, cold universe: 'I am proceeding like a heavenly body on course towards the point of destruction. My house collapses again and again in my trying to reconstruct it. Therefore, I feel despair.' This statement suggested that she had fallen out of a shared human world, the only reality where the drive-instinctual tensions can receive inner meanings.

Ms O was horrified at her vital affects and tried by any means to disavow them. Therefore, she also felt her dreams were very frightening: 'I am more horrified by my dreams than my hallucinations which I can control. My dreams are too lively.' Ultimately, her problems remained intertwined with an insurmountable anxiety. In her case, the phrase 'to be scared to death' was right: repeated suicidal attempts characterised her life history.

Ms O was extremely ambivalent about all forms of intimacy, but especially about her intimacy with other women. Therefore, only a few options were available to her to maintain her inner vitality, the most important of which was masochistic suffering, which, despite its destructiveness, offered her a narrow possibility of human interaction and psychic survival. In her case, it is easy to agree with Rudolph Loewenstein (1957), who characterised masochism as 'the weapon of the weak – i.e. of every child – faced with the danger of human aggression.'

Because it was of vital importance for my patient to experience herself as definitively independent in her relationship with me, my emotional freedom was very limited. Little by little, however, she started to evoke warm, sensual responses in me, although I felt they were completely incongruent with the strained atmosphere of the sessions. Nevertheless, I perceived a timid attachment. For a long time, I felt isolated, especially concerning my aggressive feelings. Although Ms O was an expert in provoking furious affects in her immediate surroundings, she was completely unaware of the same feelings in herself, i.e., it was a projective identification.

After a half a year of psychotherapy, she was able to leave the hospital. During this phase, she sought dental treatment and wondered why a person whose only interest was to die cared about her teeth. Knowing her biting aggression, it was not difficult for me to understand that she needed her teeth and affects to transform her inward destruction to object-directional activity. During this phase, it became possible for us to reconstruct many memories of her adolescence. Unfortunately, this period in her treatment did not last long. Within a few months Ms O began to abuse tranquillisers and regressed again into a psychotic state. After one year of psychotherapy, she had to resume hospital treatment. Before that, she had cut her hair short and disguised herself as a nun as a sign of ascetic self-renunciation.

Pain and suffering as an 'identity theme'

During the following six months, the hospital ward formed a stage for Ms O's sadomasochistic drama, in which the nurses came to represent her destructive inner mother. By contrast, I came to represent a benevolent helper, whom she tried, by all means, to manipulate against her persecutors. The daily conflicts in the ward were related to her drug use and heavy smoking, which also formed an actual danger not only to Ms O's health but to the hospital security. These problems became closely associated with her mother, who could behave very coldly and cruelly toward her daughter's vital needs while visiting her in the ward.

Simultaneously, however, a psychic integration of Ms O's acting out took place, and she became more attuned to her passionate hatred. Her oral rage became associated with her early maternal frustrations and traumatic separation. She could, for example, desperately lament:

'The people here go away. Although they hear me crying, they won't help me. Why can't they come to see me or light me a cigarette? That is the most terrible example of sadism.' At the same time, she could during her session take gulps of water from a small bottle that she was carrying with her as a concession to her inner mother and life in general.

After meeting her mother, I could understand more clearly my patient's *extreme ambivalence*. In her mother's speech, daily occurrences and paranoid delusions from the distant past occurred confusingly intertwined. Listening to her mother, I could not resist falling into a chaotic state of mind characterised by a peculiar unbound excitation as well as contradictory discharges of affect. I felt alternately like bursting into laughter and tears. When I told Ms O about my experience, she seemed relieved and said that I could finally understand her situation. Harold Searles' (1959) *The Effort to Drive Another Person Crazy* comes to my mind. If the mother's presence excites in the infant at least a somewhat comparable affect storm as mine, then it is no wonder that its helpless ego may result in self-destructive measures including a radical withdrawal of its libidinal cathexes. Ms O's early maternal impingement had manifested in the transference to the hospital ward. (Winnicott, 1974).

While Ms O hated her mother from the bottom of her heart, she simultaneously had a desperate longing for genuine intimacy with her. In referring to her ecstatic delusions, she once said: 'After such an experience, one only thinks about what one has lost. Average life has since then felt so flat that there is no idea of living any longer.' She had dreams of dying together with somebody or deceased persons becoming resurrected. All of this was not difficult to connect with her mother, whom Ms O could characterise: 'Already hearing her voice is part of my self-destruction.' In brief, death formed an all-pervasive theme in her life, rooted deeply in her primary identification. One can hardly find more convincing evidence for Freud's notion of erotogenic masochism deriving its sources from early psychic trauma.

When the hospital staff once again had to restrict Ms O's freedom to prevent her going outside of the hospital, she experienced this as an extreme narcissistic insult. Then she was finally able to express her unfathomable hate of her mother in the transference: 'You are destroying me, you kill. You are worse than a murderer.' I can't help thinking that she had 'soul murder' in mind (Shengold, 1978) i.e., the annihilation of her primary identification. After this confrontation, a pivotal change took place in our relationship. Suddenly I felt separated from her, and her relationship to me changed correspondingly. Ms O understood that her aggression was also linked to her sexuality and her erotic wishes towards me.

In the first half of the third year of psychotherapy, her psychic integration proceeded quite smoothly, and she came to realise that she had been in a state of psychotic regression for many years. She also told me about an incident in her early infancy. At the age of two months, her family had been evacuated from their native town because of the war. The father was at the front, and the mother took care of her two daughters, my patient and her sister, who was two years older. In these extreme circumstances, the infant caught a bacterial infection which led to abscesses on her skin. Her mother treated the abscesses by lancing them with a blade. Ms O believed that this painful episode had left a lasting imprint on her later relationship with her mother. We might wonder if this incident was significant in her becoming deeply addicted to pain, or whether her opinion is a derivative of later sadomasochistic fantasies related to a child's primal scene. In any case, the incident took place at a most vulnerable phase in her psychic development, corresponding to primary identification. The first alternative is supported by Betty Joseph's (1982) observation that patients who become passionately addicted to living close to death have often had some painful physical condition in their early infancy, which they try to control by persecuting themselves as well as others. Nevertheless, pain and suffering seemed to form an 'identity theme' for Ms O (Lichtenstein, 1964).

In the course of her psychic integration, Ms O's anxiety paradoxically increased. She felt a burning ache in her breast without understanding what it meant. When I expressed curiosity at why she felt pain in the breast, she remembered her unhappy engagement and her first love in adolescence. After working through these painful memories, she came to grasp the importance of her father. This phase was characterised by a fragile object love to me as the representative of the Oedipal father in the transference.

Unfortunately, this process also suffered a setback. Indeed, the arousal of hope and its catastrophic loss was a leitmotif of Ms O's inner drama, the pull of which I found difficult to resist. Once again, she attempted suicide, then fell into profound catatonic regression.

In the realm of death

Ms O took an almost fatal overdose of tranquillisers in the front door of her mother's house, but survived owing to a successful emergency treatment. After returning to the mental hospital, she was very tense, believing herself to be somatically ill. 'I am sick from the top of my hair to the toes . . . I am living in my body following its functions. It functions wrongly.' She also believed that I was in danger of contagion. Because of feeling guilty about her destructive act, she wondered how anybody could treat such a worthless person as herself.

In a few days, her regression resulted in a catatonic state endangering her vital physiological functions. It was necessary to feed her like a baby while she gazed around, fearful and alarmed. She consented to eat only when we kept assuring her that the food was not dangerous and that only people with whom she was acquainted were present. The depth of her regression was also revealed in the way that, after each mouthful, her hands made involuntary instinctive groping movements akin to an infant at its mother's breast.

In the following week, her condition began to improve. Even though she was still very timid, her gaze took on a new quality which I did not understand at the time. She was silently looking me in the eye, steadily and warmly, as if she had been asking something. When I later confronted the same unwavering gaze in another patient of mine, I suddenly understood the riddle of Ms O. Her reduced rudimentary ego had recognised in me her primary object that she had traumatically lost. At this particular moment, her psychic existence was in a nascent state, as it were. What was going on was the recovery of her primary identification in the transference.

Soon, her vitality began to fade. She began to resemble more and more a living corpse. Her entire person embodied the idea which seized her: after recovery, Ms O told me of having been in the 'realm of death' and no longer in her body. Regardless of the collapse of her entire representational world, she had all the time recognised me and felt the feeding procedure at the hospital ward as a bond with reality.

Ms O's psychotic regression was not only indicative of the decathexis of her internal object world, but also her vital physiological functions that had lost their life-sustaining preconscious significance for her. In fact, her hypochondriacal sensations can be seen as the ultimate defence of her rudimentary ego, before she was left at the mercy of crude drive-energetic discharge without hope and consolation.

By these kinds of clinical observations, I am inclined to think that even an almost complete decathexis of the representational world does not necessarily form an absolute obstacle to the recovery of primary identification. It is quite another matter if the patient still has drive-instinctual resources to return to a shared human reality. In this respect, a psychotic state resembles a severe psychosomatic disorder: in both cases, a giving up of hope, indicating the depletion of the primary narcissistic resources at the ego's disposal.

Epilogue

After recovering from her life-threatening condition, Ms O's psychotherapy proceeded in an atmosphere of greater autonomy. In this phase, she became warmly attached to a female older than herself. Unfortunately, this relationship also repeated the fateful constellation imprinted in Ms O's primary identification. After half a year, this friend committed suicide after first discussing her plan with my patient. Later Ms O told me that they had in passing also discussed a double suicide, which naturally aroused intolerable feelings of guilt in Ms O. Perhaps Freud's notion of fate neurosis, *Schicksalzwang*, was based on such clinical observations.

A short phase of mourning followed Ms O's fateful loss, during which she was more integrated than ever since falling ill. Her friend's destructive act had confronted her harshly with the ultimate realities of life. Ms O was able to grasp her friend's significance for herself, but not her ambivalent feelings towards her friend, let alone the destructive potential in their relationship from the first beginnings. When Ms O was finally capable of depending on another human being without abandoning her friend, she was traumatically deserted. Ms O's heartrending sorrow was linked with many other losses as well, not least falling ill at the threshold of adulthood, the meaning of which she could clearly realise.

However, the final integration of her painful loss proved to be an overwhelming task. In a few months, her sincere mourning transformed into destructive disavowal. When idealising her friend's destructive solution, she disavowed her genuine dependence on another human being, including the therapeutic relationship. As a result, her frail object ties dissolved, and she was left at the mercy of her crude aggression discharged through an archaic superego, whereas her ego became a triumphant executor of her fate. Without telling me about her real intention, she established an eroticised relationship with a manic man with whom she was planning her suicide. No ambivalence was perceptible in her final decision, and no space was left for completing her work of mourning in the therapeutic setting. Through the clinical material presented above, we can perhaps understand why the psychic integration of her ambivalence formed for Ms O a greater danger than her actual death.

An additional remark

Regardless of the opinion, an individual psychoanalyst has on the concept of the death drive; it is essential to understand that in *Beyond the Pleasure Principle*, Freud (1920) focused on destructive drive phenomena that remain outside the sphere of psychic representation. To visualise this point clearly, I would like to return to Harry Martinsson's (1963) epic poem *Aniara, A Review of Man in Space and Time*, forming a crucial reference for my understanding of the voids of psychic representation (Titelman, 2016).

The fate of *Aniara*, a spaceship thrown from its regular course into the infinite universe and destined to proceed with its travellers on a never-ending trajectory towards destruction, evokes Freud's two modalities of psychic regulation, the pleasure principle and beyond. Repetition compulsion, the 'demonic force' described by Freud represents, paradoxically, also a drive-instinctual tendency to restore psychic functioning to its regular course, i.e. to navigation according to the pleasure principle within the metaphorical space of primary identification. That this corrective manoeuvre implies a risk depends on whether the libidinal resources available to the ego are commensurable with unbound aggression eluding psychic representation and, on the other hand, with the capability for the work of mourning, enabling a balanced distribution of libidinal resources and aggression within an individual's psychic organisation.

Note

1 This paper was originally published in *Scand. Psychoanal. Rev.*, 29: 72–80 (2006). Copyright© The Psychoanalytic Societies of Denmark, Finland, Norway, and Sweden, reprinted by permission of Taylor & Francis Ltd, www.tandfonline.com on behalf of The Psychoanalytic Societies of Denmark, Finland, Norway, and Sweden.

References

Eissler, K.R. (1971). Death Drive, Ambivalence, and Narcissism. *Psychoanal. St. Child*, 26:25–78

Enckell, H. (2002). *Metaphor and the Psychodynamic Function of the Mind.* Kuopio: Kuopio University Publications D. Medical Sciences 265.

Federn, P. (1956). *Ich-Psychologie und Psychosen.* Bern und Stuttgart: Verlag Hans Huber.

Fenichel, O. (1945). *The Psychoanalytic Theory of Neurosis.* London: Routledge and Kegan Paul Ltd.

Freud, A. (1972). Comments on aggression. *Int. J. Psychoanal.*, 53: 163–171.

Freud, S. (1915). Repression. In *The Standard Edition of the Complete Psychological Works of Sigmund Freud*, Volume XIV. London: The Hogarth Press and the Institute of Psychoanalysis, pp. 141–158.

Freud, S. (1920). Beyond the pleasure principle. In *The Standard Edition of the Complete Psychological Works of Sigmund Freud*, Volume XVIII. London: The Hogarth Press and the Institute of Psychoanalysis, pp. 1–64.

Freud, S. (1924). The economic problem of masochism. In *The Standard Edition of the Complete Psychological Works of Sigmund Freud*, Volume XIX. London: The Hogarth Press and the Institute of Psychoanalysis, pp. 155–170.

Freud, S. (1930). Civilization and its discontents. In *The Standard Edition of the Complete Psychological Works of Sigmund Freud*, Volume XXI. London: The Hogarth Press and the Institute of Psychoanalysis, pp. 64–145.

Gaddini, E. (1972). Aggression and the pleasure principle: Towards a psychoanalytic theory of aggression. In *A Psychoanalytic Theory of Infantile Experience.* Limentani, A. (editor). London and New York: Tavistock: Routledge, 1992, pp. 35–45.

Ikonen, P. and Rechardt, E. (1978). The vicissitudes of thanatos. *Scand. Psychoanal. Rev.*, 1: 79–114.

Ikonen, P. and Rechardt, E. (1993). How to interpret the death drive. *Scand. Psychoanal. Rev.*, 16: 84–99.

Joseph, B. (1982). Addiction to near-death. *Int. J. Psychoanal.*, 63: 449–456.

Klein, M. (1948). A contribution to the theory of anxiety and guilt. *Int. J. Psychoanal.*, 29: 114–123.

Laplanche, J. (1976). *Life and Death in Psychoanalysis.* Baltimore, MD and London: The Johns Hopkins University Press.

Lichtenstein, H. (1964). The role of narcissism in the emergence and maintenance of a primary identity. *Int. J. Psychoanal.*, 45: 49–56.

Lind, L. (1991). Thanatos: The drive without a name. The development of the concept of the death drive in Freud's writings. *Scand. Psychoanal. Rev.*, 14: 60–80.

Loewenstein, R. (1957). A contribution to the psychoanalytic theory of masochism. *J. Amer. Psychoanal. Assn.*, 5: 197–234.

Martinsson, H. (1963). *Aniara, a Review of Man in Space and Time*. Adapted from the Swedish by Hugh MacDiarmid and Elizabeth Harley Schubert. London: Hutchinson Co. Ltd.

Rangell, L. (1967). Psychoanalysis, affects, and the "human core". *Psychoanal. Q.*, 36: 172–202.

Rosenfeld, H. (1971). A clinical approach to the psychoanalytic theory of the life and death instincts: An investigation into the aggressive aspects of narcissism. *Int. J. Psychoanal.*, 52: 169–178.

Schur, M. (1972). *Freud: Living and Dying*. New York: Int. Univ. Press, p. 332.

Searles, H. F. (1959). The effort to drive the other person crazy. *Brit. J. Med. Psychol.*, 32: 1–18.

Shengold, L. (1978). Assault on a child's individuality: A kind of soul murder. *Psychoanal. Q.*, 47: 419–424.

Stein, R. (1991). *Psychoanalytic Theories of Affect*. London: Karnac Books.

Titelman, D. (2016). Harry Martinson: The destination of a master writer. A paper read at the *25th Nordic Psychoanalytic Congress*, Stockholm, 4–7 August.

Torsti-Hagman, M. (2003). *Harvesting Free Association*. London: Free Association Books.

Winnicott, D. W. (1974). *Playing and Reality*. Harmondsworth: Penguin Books.

10

THE BODY AND THE SENSE OF REALITY[1]

In Finnish, the word for body is *ruumis*, which contains antithetical meanings since it can refer both to a living and to a deceased person. Only the context of the word reveals which meaning is intended. To eliminate this ambiguity, a neologism *keho* was invented, to refer explicitly to a living person. But after a period of seventy years this word has not established itself completely, and is used more often to refer to superficial or artificial contexts, for example, 'body building'. Deeper emotional meanings are elicited by the word *ruumis*, which contains both aspects of life and lifelessness (Hägglund and Piha, 1979). This ambiguity is not only a linguistic question but reflects a deeper ambivalence in the individual's relation to death and dying, perhaps the same ambivalence Freud approached in his later drive theory. Furthermore, I propose that the psychic integration of this ambivalence will also restore a living contact with one's body and vital affects.

René Spitz (1972) derived the origins of our sense of reality from the non-verbal dialogue between the infant and its mother. Via this interaction, the child's elemental psychic movements find a living response in the mother and vice versa. The child acquires a capacity to differentiate between living and inanimate objects during the second half of the first year of life and thus is able to orient himself accordingly. Spitz sees life as a kind of a dialogue reaching new stages of psychic integration. A familiar human face, having already disappeared, can be rediscovered in new contexts, thus signifying a re-vitalisation of the affect experience. In the following discussion, I am going to examine the sense of reality as a process of integration within a frame of reference originally established in the bodily intimacy between infant and mother. Before delving more deeply into this subject, I will analyse the links between the body and mind from another vantage point.

On the vital preconditions of psychic functioning

In his *On Narcissism: An Introduction* (1914), Freud proposed that the understanding of schizophrenia and somatic disorders should shed additional light on the theoretical problems which cannot be solved solely from the viewpoint of transference neurosis. Subsequent our clinical experience has considerably added to the understanding of this area, but we are still faced with many difficulties. Although the pathological conditions mentioned by Freud illuminate the foundations of psychic functioning, they nonetheless still tend to elude a solid psychoanalytic understanding based on inner meanings. How can we understand phenomena beyond primal repression, which our psychotic and psychosomatic patients try to express in their fragmented way? I think we still have no other choice but to resort to metapsychological extrapolations in the hope that the results of our scientific journey would conform to the solid corpus of psychoanalytic knowledge and the ordinary experiences of everyday life.

To explore this topic, we have to put ourselves in the place of an infant without psychic representations striving for orientation in the early human environment. All the infant has are bodily sensations and excitations through which it approaches and attempts to interact with the world. In this hypothetical beginning of psychic development, the infant has no frame of reference to cope with its sensory-motor responses and drive-instinctual urges. In this inchoate state, it is not justified to speak of drive-instinctual wishes either. Only later on will these wishes link the infant to human reality. The early maternal environment becomes real for the infant insofar as it offers relief from pain and distress, i.e., from traumatic excitation. This relief is also the aim of the drive-instinctual wishes through which the bodily excitations receive preliminary psychic meanings.

By imagining the infant's excitement at the mother's breast, we can grasp Freud's idea that the child's entire body functions as a sense organ. According to Freud, the individual's vital narcissistic interests in life are rooted in this excitement in the same way as the object libidinal interests are rooted in the maternal feeding. Freud's notion of *Anlehnung* refers to the instinctual drives leaning on the vital bodily functions (Laplanche and Pontalis, 1973, pp. 29–32).

I would like to discuss an additional aspect of Freud's famous work, namely the question of primary narcissism. This notion not only refers to the preliminary distribution of psychic intensities in the infant but also opens a larger developmental perspective to psychoanalytic theory. Freud outlines a primary narcissistic resource or reservoir, from which both object-libidinal and narcissistic interests then evolve. Primary narcissism corresponds to the state of self-sufficient pleasure and perfection, which is not possible to separate from the infant's bodily wellbeing. According to Freud, this state of perfection does not disappear without trace during psychic development but will be retained in the capacity of the ego-ideal. Thus, it not only forms a vital starting point for psychic development but also extends to the future as an ideal to become attained.

To understand in more detail the processes in the background of normal psychic functioning, we should examine an interesting paper by Freud's contemporary, Viktor Tausk, from 1919. He described a common delusion entertained by the schizophrenic patients of his time, namely that they have fallen under the influence of a mystical device or machine. Tausk presented the case of Miss Natalija A, whose delusion was remarkably complex. Following the approach of dream interpretation, Tausk first assumed that the patient was trying to control her unconscious sexual wishes by projecting them onto the outside world. Accordingly, the mystical device was understood to represent the excited sexual organ persistently disturbing the patient. Transcending this analysis, Tausk then proposed that the influencing machine represented the patient's body and its different functions, which are experienced as belonging to the outside world in the same way as an infant originally perceives his body before recognising it as belonging to himself through primary identification:

> The projection of one's body may, then, be traced back to the developmental stage in which one's own body is the goal of the object finding. This must be the time when the infant is discovering his body, part by part, as the outer world, and is still groping for his hands and feet as though they were foreign objects. At this time, everything that "happens" to him emanates from his own body; his psyche is the object of stimuli arising in his own body but acting upon it as if produced by outer objects. These *disjecta membra* are

later on pieced together and systematized into a unified whole under the supervision of a psychic unity that receives all sensations of pleasure and pain from these separate parts. This process takes place by means of identification with one's own body. The ego, thus discovered, is cathected with the available libido; in accordance with the psychic nature of the ego, narcissism develops; and, in accordance with the function of individual organs as sources of pleasure, autoeroticism results.

(1933, pp. 541–542)

In this way, the human body and its various functions acquire a vital narcissistic meaning through primary identification. According to Tausk, this also signifies an individual's attachment to life. This simple but fundamental viewpoint has escaped notice in psychoanalytic discussion, which may emphasise, perhaps one-sidedly, the importance of object relations for psychic survival. My aim is to demonstrate that the primal narcissistic interest in the body and its functions plays a crucial part in an individual's psychic and somatic survival. What is at stake here is the drive-instinctual basis of confidence in life. According to Krystal (1978), the collapse of this basis signifies extreme traumatic helplessness and the greatest conceivable horror, *Todesangst*.

Two clinical examples

I am going to illustrate this state of extreme distress with two clinical cases, both of which related to a psychosomatic emergency. The first of my patients, Ms K, had undergone a radical colon resection because of a fulminant ulcerative colitis that had become acute after her divorce. In that connection, she had experienced an agonising ambivalence and loyalty conflict related to her children (Wurmser, 1988).

When we met the first time, Ms K's condition was critical. The wounds from the operation were not healing. On the contrary, they were severely infected, resulting in several fistulae in her body. The idea of integrating an aspect of psychotherapy into her treatment emerged as a result of her having lost all interest in her recovery. The other reason for asking me to join the hospital staff was to refine the therapeutic approach in this emergency.

Ms K's somatic treatment consisted of a continuous monitoring of her vital functions, hour-by-hour and week-by-week. Especially her extensive skin lesions demanded treatment analogous to the physical care of an infant. As a result of the supreme efforts of the hospital staff, her grave condition stabilised. My responsibility during this phase was primarily to represent, through my recurrent presence, temporal continuity in the therapeutic setting. Ms K was not all the time aware of my role in her treatment.

When she was recovering, a new crisis occurred. To be sure that her healing was proceeding well, an endoscopy was necessary. Ms K's sense of reality was at that time still so shaky she misunderstood this operation as a malignant invasion of her body. As a result, her physical condition also deteriorated, and intensive treatment procedures had to be resumed. After surviving her life-threatening somatic condition, Ms K started psychotherapy with me, one session per week, for almost five years. She was never interested in increasing the number of her sessions. A paralysing despair associated with the colostomy on her abdominal wall characterised our relationship.

Ms K was not able to control her bowel movements. Correspondingly, her affect experience was in a state of dispersion. It was 'leaking' too. A radical change in her treatment took place after the surgical reconstruction of a reservoir in her body, equipped with a valve allowing her to voluntarily control the bowel function, thus replacing the missing rectal and anal functions. It was quite evident that an identification with her reconstructed somatic function restored Ms K's confidence in her body and led subsequently and dramatically to her recovering her affect control as well, consonant with Freud's notion of *Anlehnung*. After restoring the bodily preconditions of normal psychic functioning, Ms K was able to face her agonising ambivalence, instead of resorting to denial and succumbing to paralysing despair. In short, she recovered her confidence in life. In concluding her therapy, she also was able to integrate the cosmetic defects as a result of her illness into a feminine self-image without their leaving any uncontrolled masochistic 'leakage' in her psychic economy.

My second clinical example, Ms R, sought help in her sixties for a psychotic depression. She suffered from a delusion that her digestive system was damaged and that she therefore could not eat. She had lost weight at an alarming rate. I understood the strange train of her thought as an abortive attempt to digest metaphorically a tragic loss in the distant past: her little daughter's unexpected death from a respiratory infection. Like all melancholic persons, she tried to deal with her loss in oral-incorporative terms – to digest it concretely– without her conflict finding a metaphorical solution. Therefore, she felt destruction and death threatening her from inside.

Once again, Ms R had a compelling need to undergo physical examinations. This time it was possible to find a very simple explanation for her strange bodily sensations. The elongated aorta was compressing her oesophagus, which made it difficult for her to swallow. This malformation was related to her age and did not demand a surgical operation. Instead, she received a realistic medical explanation for her bodily sensations, whereas they had previously supported her delusional interpretation. After this discovery, a dramatic change also took place in Ms R's treatment. In a short time, her confidence in the normal functioning of her body was restored, thus leading to the recovery of her affect experience as well. It is difficult to imagine that this could have been attained without first working through her painful loss, which took place on the stage of her life also normally presupposing a new integration through the work of mourning.

Analogous to these two clinical cases is that of recovering from heart surgery. A surgical intervention in this area may prove to be a shattering experience, the psychic integration of which may signify a profound reorientation in life. In the same way, the recovery of a cancer patient may demand a long period of working through after the illness itself is in remission. Before attaining this goal, it may be necessary to deal with destructive phantasies the patient himself tries to control through magical thoughts and omnipotent beliefs. Given this fusional state of helplessness, it is not easy to differentiate between one's phantasy and bodily functions (Salonen, 1997). Undifferentiated thinking then offers a temporary retreat from the painful realities of life, the preconscious meanings of which are still too painful to integrate. In these situations, the analyst's task is to represent the temporal continuity of psychic experience. The analytic setting creates the preconditions necessary for integrating these meanings as well as the painful affects related to them as an intrinsic part of an individual's life.

Primary identification and psychic representation

Freud's notion of primary identification has caused difficulties for later generations of analysts because he maintained that it preceded ordinary object ties (Freud, 1923). Most psychoanalysts are inclined to see primary identification as synonymous with early maternal fusion, without this concept having any structural connotations.

The body and the sense of reality

Viktor Tausk's paper quoted above clarifies this problem by linking it to object finding, including finding one's body and its functions.

Gaddini (1987) associated the emergence of the first psychic configuration with the infant's bodily contact with the mother. He called this formation BMO, the *basic mental organisation*. Green (1986) correspondingly suggested that the maternal fusion object does not disappear without a trace, but will form a framing structure for psychic representation. Through primary identification, the infant acquires an inner frame of reference, within the confines of which bodily responses become transposed to the psychic level as vital affects and preconscious psychic meanings, analogous to Bion's (1963, 1965) container function. As projected onto the future, this configuration also delineates the ego–ideal, which is consonant with Freud's original definition of primary identification.

The functional modality of primary identification does not disappear with the advance of psychic development (Sandler, 1993). As a mode of object finding, it plays a major role in configuring individual psychic existence. The original human frame of reference will be rediscovered over and over again in new contexts as if it were occurring for the first time. A new integration of reality will never be a mere application of the previous one. Hence, we return to Spitz's idea of life as a dialogue involving ever-new stages of integration.

The continuation of an inner dialogue with the primary object is not self-evident but presupposes an integrated psychic organisation, which is not always the case. Those patients suffering from serious problems in this area may help us to understand the nature of primary identification. I have in mind a young hebephrenic man, whom I treated over six years three times a week in a hospital. The following episode is from his treatment, already dealt with in the second chapter of this book.

On entering my office, Eli's person seemed deeply fragmented. His skin was grey, and his gaze seemed dim in a way that originally lead me to approach schizophrenia as a decathexis of the primal representative matrix (Salonen, 1979). What especially struck me was the lifelessness of Eli's mouth area. The motor co-ordination of his tongue seemed to be disorganised. After a long silence, he said in a harsh and toneless voice: 'This room is a crack, let's go to another room.' Intuitively, I decided to follow his wish. We left my dark office and moved into the bright hospital library. The atmosphere of the session was suddenly transformed. His entire being became bright and his voice clear. Then, it was possible for us to discuss his thoughts in sharp contrast to the deep fragmentation of his entire person.

How can we explain Eli's quick recovery? This question can be answered by thinking about the bright room representing the healthy aspect of his primary identification. What seemed to happen was the recognition of a lost primary object in the transference. Eli's fragmented sentence 'this room is a crack, let's go to another room', reflects the fragmented aspect of his primary identification and his wish for recovery. It should be mentioned that Eli's mother had been psychotic when he was a child, so he was exposed to the 'crack' in the mother's mind. The mother represents for her child the frame for an intuitive understanding, comparable to the sounding board of a musical instrument (Piha, 2005). As a consequence of his defective psychic development, Eli was unable to attain a sound psychic integration.

Eli's episode sheds additional light on another issue regarding the mind-body continuum, namely his physical appearance, indicating the collapse of his psychic functioning on the elementary level. This is consonant with Leo Rangell's (1954) view that the motor expression of the perioral region reflects the individual's original wellbeing at the mother's breast. Eli's oral responses were disorganised after losing their life-sustaining preconscious meaning. Through these observations, we can ask to what extent the vital bodily functions lean on psychic integrity and not only *vice versa*. Recent neurophysiological observations of breast-feeding infants support this hypothesis (Lehtonen, 1997; Lehtonen *et al.*, 2006). The feeding situation seems to configure the brain function too.

The pain of psychic integration

Primary identification originally configures an inner constellation that Joyce McDougall (1989) characterised as 'one body for two'. However, the infant's psychic survival presupposes individuation within the frame of this constellation, which may prove too painful. When this pain, which cannot be distinguished from bodily pain, becomes associated with the idea of castration, this idea may receive an agonising intensity. In this case, castration not only signifies the loss of one's genital integrity, but also the deprivation of one's primary narcissistic well-being and autoerotic pleasures. McDougall's observation that psychosomatic patients may prefer even dying of somatic causes to the painful process of psychic integration is consonant with this view. However, the psychic integration of this agony through Oedipal solutions forms a narrow gateway to the rediscovery of the body at the genital level of psychic organisation.

Freud's (1940) insight into the fetish as a final implementation of the ego split can be understood from this perspective. By inventing a fetish, the ego adheres to the still undifferentiated image of the phallic mother to disavow the idea of castration and the significance of the father in the primal scene (Chasseguet-Smirgel, 1981, 1985). Instead of genuine object love, the ego becomes addicted to a lifeless substitute, the fetish, and hence engages in compulsive efforts to animate it by autoerotic excitation and blind idealisation. A precarious psychic coherence is gained on the undifferentiated level of psychic organisation. What is lost is contact with one's libidinal wishes and vital affects that evolve only in genuine bodily intimacy.

Let us return to my starting point: the ambivalence towards one's body in the face of the drive-instinctual dangers of separation, castration, and the loss of love. Instead of integrating this ambivalence, the fetishistic solution aims at eliminating it by adopting a lifeless object as an idol. This not only leads to a split in reality perception, but also to the stagnation of a living dialogue with the lost primary object on the metaphorical level of psychic processes.

The crux of individual psychic development is attaining the genital level of psychic integration through Oedipal solutions. This signifies not only a painful surrender of infantile sexual aims and narcissistic ambitions but also the discovery of one's sexual body in adolescence at a new stage of psychic integration, which implies the capability for autonomous use of one's body not only for the acts of love but also for the acts of real destruction. This integration of an individual's fundamental ambivalence involves the conditions necessary for the continuation of a living dialogue at the level of primary identification, despite the drive-instinctual dangers inherent in human life.

A temporal perspective

When Marion M. Oliner (1996) analysed the concept of external reality in psychoanalysis, she pointed to the fact that this concept has been customarily associated with superego demands as a counterpoint to drive-instinctual wishes, which has then led to the neglect of another aspect of reality, namely the actual relief and consolation it may offer. This also applies to the reality of time and the mortal body, being outside the illusion of one's omnipotent control.

We can now return to my starting point. To understand that the living body is the same entity that some day will die and become buried not only signifies a resignation in facing reality, but also a sense of actual relief in renouncing the unconscious belief in one's omnipotence and perfection. The body will then become rediscovered at a new stage of psychic integration, which not only means revitalisation of affect experience but also identification with one's contemporaries, as well as a renewed interest in life.

In conclusion, I would like to refer to Peter Hartocollis' (1976) work on the experience of time. Hartocollis approached this question from two different aspects, namely, the subjective duration of time, depending on drive-instinctual expectations at the moment and the experience of time as a perspective in life. According to him, the latter refers to an affect state that transcends the basic modality of pleasure *versus* unpleasure in individual life. I have attempted to show that this perspective is linked with the body, implying a shadow, namely the preconscious knowledge that one's time is limited, of which the body is the most faithful reminder, thus forming an interface to reality on the metaphorical level.

Note

1 The paper was read at the 6th Delphi International Psychoanalytic Symposium held in Delphi, Greece in October 2004, and published as a shorter version in *Beyond the Mind-Body Dualism: Psychoanalysis and the Human Body*. Zacharacopoulou, E. (editor). Elsevier International Congress Series #1286, pp. 33–40 (2006). Copyright© 2005 Elsevier B.V. Reprinted by permission of Elsevier.

References

Bion, W. R. (1963). *Elements of Psychoanalysis*. London: William Heinemann Medical Books.

Bion, W. R. (1965). *Transformations*. London: William Heinemann Medical Books.

Chasseguet-Smirgel, J. (1981). Loss of reality in perversions – with special reference to fetishism. *J. Amer. Psychoanal. Assn.*, 29: 511–534.

Chasseguet-Smirgel, J. (1985). *Creativity and Perversion*. London: Free Association Books.

Freud, S. (1914). On narcissism. In *The Standard Edition of the Complete Psychological Works of Sigmund Freud*, Volume XIV. London: The Hogarth Press and the Institute of Psychoanalysis, pp. 67–102.

Freud, S. (1923). The ego and the id. In *The Standard Edition of the Complete Psychological Works of Sigmund Freud*, Volume XIX. London: The Hogarth Press and the Institute of Psychoanalysis, pp. 1–66.

Freud, S. (1940). Splitting of the ego in the process of defence. In *The Standard Edition of the Complete Psychological Works of Sigmund Freud*, Volume XXIII. London: The Hogarth Press and the Institute of Psychoanalysis, pp. 271–278.

Gaddini, E. (1987). Notes on the mind – body question. *Int. J. Psychoanal.*, 68: 315–329.

Green, A. (1986). The dead mother. In *On Private Madness*. London: The Hogarth Press and the Institute of Psychoanalysis, pp. 142–173. Reference to *Narcissisme vie: Narcissisme de mort*. Paris: Minuit, 1983.

Hägglund, T.-B. and Piha, H. (1979). *Ruumiinkuvan sisätila, psykoanalyyttisia näkökohtia*. Reports from Psychiatria Fennica 37.

Hartocollis, P. (1976). On the experience of time and its dynamics, with special reference to affects. *J. Amer. Psychoanal. Assn.*, 24: 363–375.

Krystal, H. (1978). Trauma and affects. *Psychoanal. Study Child*, 33: 81–116.

Laplanche, J. and Pontalis, J.-B. (1973). *The Language of Psychoanalysis*. New York: W. W. Norton, pp. 29–32.

Lehtonen, J. (1997). On the origins of the body ego and its implications for psychotic vulnerability. In *Seed of Madness: Constitution, Environment, and Fantasy in the Organization of the Psychotic Core*. Volkan, V. D. and Akhtar, S. (editors). Madison, CT: Int. Univ. Press, pp. 19–58.

Lehtonen, J., Partanen, J., Purhonen, M., Valkonen-Korhonen, M., Kononen, M., Saarikoski, S. and Launiala, K. (2006). Nascent body ego: Metapsychological and neurophysiological aspects. *Int. J. Psychoanal.*, 87: 1335–1353.

McDougall, J. (1989). *Theaters of the Body: A Psychoanalytical Approach to Psychosomatic Illness*. New York and London: W. W. Norton.

Oliner, M. M. (1996). External reality: The elusive dimension of psychoanalysis. *Psychoanal. Q.*, 65: 267–301.

Piha, H. (2005). Intuition: A bridge to the coenesthetic world of experience. *J. Amer. Psychoanal. Assn.*, 53: 23–49.

Rangell, L. (1954). The psychology of poise – with a special elaboration on the psychic significance of the snout or perioral region. *Int. J. Psychoanal.*, 35: 313–332.

Salonen, S. (1979). On the metapsychology of schizophrenia. *Int. J. Psychoanal.*, 60: 73–81.

Salonen, S. (1997). Humiliation and dignity: Reflections on ego integrity. In *Seed of Madness: Constitution, Environment, and Fantasy in the Organization* of the Psychotic Core. Volkan, V. D. and Akhtar, S. (editors). Madison, CT: Int. Univ. Press, pp. 59–79.

Sandler, J. (1993). On communication from patient to analyst: Not everything is projective identification. *Int. J. Psychoanal.*, 74: 1097–1107.

Spitz, R. A. (1972). Das Leben und der Dialog. *Psyche – Z. Psychoanal.*, 26: 249–264.

Tausk, V. (1933). On the origin of the "influencing machine" in schizophrenia. *Psychoanal. Q.*, 2: 519–556.

Wurmser, L. (1988). "The sleeping giant": A dissenting comment about borderline pathology. *Psychoanal. Inquiry*, 8: 373–397.

11

THE ABSENT FATHER IN THE TRANSFERENCE

A case study of primary identification and psychic survival[1]

Martin contacted me over thirty years ago to begin psychoanalysis. He felt unable to cope with his profession as a teacher, as he suffered greatly from conflicts with his colleagues. He also talked about uncomfortable sensations in his genital area and a painful restlessness in his body. He had recently consulted a surgeon to assure himself that his penis was intact. It became evident that he had suffered from the same complaints fifteen years earlier after he started dating his future wife. In those days, he had been sexually fearful and shy. In the same way, starting his psychoanalysis elicited sexual fears, the ultimate sources of which were in his early infancy.

The immediate cause for seeking analytic help was a conflict with his supervisor at work, who in many ways represented a father figure and against whom Martin appeared to have rebelled without being clearly conscious of it. Another important episode took place two weeks after beginning his treatment. Martin became furious with a neighbour after she had accused his son of some minor mischief. Once again, he had strange sensations in his lower body and conscious thoughts of being castrated. When Martin came back to this episode later in the analysis, he mentioned that he had perhaps also heard the voice of his mother, which indicated, according to him, that his inner mother had been destroyed.

At our first meeting, Martin was in his early forties and had a good job after completing his academic studies. He was also the father of three children. The fourth child, a daughter, was born during his analysis. His choice of vocation was based on his identification with a former teacher, who had recognised his talent and supported him. This teacher also came to represent an important father figure, as Martin had never met his biological father.

As a result of his mother's inability to provide a home, Martin was placed in a children's home after he left the maternity ward, which his mother visited regularly. At the age of one he lived in his mother's childhood home under the care of his grandmother and eldest aunt. His mother, a factory worker, was at the time living in a nearby town and visited him on weekends. An uncle and an adult male cousin lived in the same household until they had to go to war. Martin remembered how disappointed he was when these worthy men returned home, physically and mentally broken. Later, the uncle fell ill with schizophrenia and was placed in a mental hospital.

Due to the mother's lack of social skills and her feelings of shame she never introduced the father of her son to him, although they lived in the same town. During his analysis, Martin finally summoned up the courage to contact his father. This was the first time the father was told he had a son. However, Martin's mother had told her son to demand monetary restitution from his father when he became an adult. This claim for compensation was to become an important theme in the transference towards the end of the analysis.

Despite childhood poverty, Martin's home offered a minimum of psychic resources for him to overcome the emotional deprivation of the first year of his life. He was loved by an array of mother figures including his own mother and his aunts. An elder aunt represented a pre-Oedipal caretaker, whereas the mother's younger sister came to represent the Oedipal mother with whom he later shared a lively interest in literature. A more integrated image and sound memory of his mother were painfully reconstructed in the analysis.

At the age of ten, Martin moved to a town where he shared a small flat with his mother and her younger aunt. This signified a remarkable expansion of his social horizon. The shy country boy found many friends and was appreciated by his new classmates as a kind and helpful humourist. However, his psychosexual identity was predominantly feminine and shadowed by his feelings of shame. On the one hand Martin was continually looking for his father among the men he met in town; on the other hand, he was anxious about meeting him, as he felt the absent father threatened his manliness.

Despite his ambivalence, Martin was able to get married and become the father of four children himself. Because his new family constellation had many similarities to his childhood family, his marriage appeared at first to function well. The threat came from within. He had great difficulties coping with his unbound drive-instinctual impulses, which resulted from his early psychic trauma and overshadowed his whole life.

His search for his father in the transference served to strengthen not only his fragile Oedipal identifications but also his psychic coherence at the pre-Oedipal level: that is, the wish to be rescued from a bottomless intrapsychic fusion with his inner mother. The collapse of this wish signified for Martin extreme helplessness against which he defended himself with paranoid projections. In short, all this made Martin extremely vulnerable in his relationships with men.

An additional aspect of his life needs to be considered, namely his interest in foreign languages, which also affected his struggle for psychic survival. Foreign languages supported his inner 'mother tongue', which he felt was in danger of psychotic fragmentation; however, through linguistic reconstructions, he attempted to reach the realm of his early psychic trauma. That he was knowledgeable in the classical languages and cultures of antiquity was intellectually stimulating in our mutual 'excavation' of his personal antiquity in the analytic setting. In this context, Martin also talked about his 'father tongue', inevitably evoking the conceptual language of Freudian metapsychology, which also represents an attempt to comprehend unrepresented psychic reality beyond ordinary language.

During the first year of analysis, we met five times a week and after that four times a week. His analysis lasted for five years. However, we resumed work fifteen years later, when we met for another five-year period, albeit less frequently. What transpired in this final period provides the key to understanding Martin's psychoanalysis.

The course of the psychoanalysis

Martin's early maternal deprivation was in the foreground during the first two years of his treatment. The holiday breaks were particularly difficult for him because of his ego-regression. Anticipating this, I provided him with an opportunity to contact me by mail. During the first holiday break, he lamented in his letters his desolate loneliness and the depletion of his vital psychic resources. On the other

The absent father in transference

hand, as an indicator of his struggle for psychic survival, he began taking swimming lessons for the first time in his life. Martin had never learned to swim as he was unable to trust water.

The resumption of our analytic work did not alleviate Martin's inconsolable anaclitic depression. On the contrary, his condition became worse, and towards the end of the first year he had to stay for a short period at a psychiatric hospital. It took almost two years for him to be able to return to his teaching position.

In the second year of analysis, he began little by little to understand that there was an analogy between his calamitous situation at the time being and the first year of his life. Before the second summer holidays, Martin had a dream where a dead child came back to life. He worried about how to cope with the future break: 'My inner mother feeling is too feeble. Therefore, I cannot survive without a father.' In the following session, he returned to the conflict with his supervisor before the beginning of his analysis: 'He was my true father. He took care of me ... at least I believed that he did. In the end, he had interests of his own, and he turned his back on me.' I said that he felt like a son deserted by his father. He responded: 'That is why masturbation also proved to be so fateful in my case.'

During his second summer vacation, Martin was able to think about me with a sense of temporal continuity. At this point he also called his father for the first time. Martin wrote to me: 'I have probably succeeded in maintaining a delicate desire in my child's heart.' At the same time, he was terrified of sexual intimacy: 'When I approach my wife, something about my mother comes to me. Afraid of meeting with my father, I try to return to mother. To place me there would, however, signify an ultimate catastrophe.' In the course of Martin's analysis, it became evident that this catastrophe was associated to his primal scene and the idea of drowning in his mother's genitals, but not only that. It was also connected with his unconscious wish to meet his father in the very concrete site of his parent's love life: his mother's genital. Martin's abysmal regression reminds us of Janine Chasseguet-Smirgel's (1988) paper on the archaic matrix of the Oedipus complex, which she elucidated in terms of bodily fusion with the mother: the unconscious wish to return to the mother's womb.

After the second summer break, we explored further the father's role in protecting his son against this fusion. At the same time, another danger occurred in Martin's dreams and associations, namely the threat of homosexual penetration. These associations were often linked with his childhood family, primarily his cousin who represented for him not only masculine strength but also sadistic violence. In the transference, these themes we embedded in a dream where a doctor drew a picture of the male genitals for protection against early maternal fusion.

Towards the end of the second year, sadistic impulses came to the fore with compelling force and centred around Martin's thoughts about Oscar Wilde's (1891) *The Picture of Dorian Gray*. These impulses became associated with his elder aunt, who had taken care of him as a child. Now she was presented as a repulsive woman. He said in adolescence he had wished to kill her, while waiting for his mother to come home.

Associated with his sadistic fantasies, Martin's regression deepened. He neglected his hygiene and lost weight. His complexion and especially his mouth seemed more and more lifeless, a sign of severe oral deprivation in early infancy (Rangell, 1954). When I confronted him with these changes, he related them to his mother and said he was living only to die. I proceeded by asking him if the present bodily changes were connected to his withdrawal from other people. Martin lamented that he had never been able to share his fears, loneliness, and worries about his body with his mother: 'Why can't we, at last, remove these black serpents from my mind?' It was the first time I as Martin's analyst was able to enter into his mother's situation and understand her helplessness about her infant. In the following session, I returned to their shared helplessness, which evoked associations with his wife: 'but with her I have captured glimpses of the same joy that I lost as a child when my mother left for town on Mondays'. Martin felt whole at that moment and was wondering why he had never before understood the psychological nature of his physical symptoms.

Unfortunately, Martin's glimpse of structural integrity did not rest on a stable foundation. His early trauma escalated in the transference during the first half of the third year. Martin bitterly lamented his hopeless starting points in his life, and alarmingly continued to lose weight. He seemed to be starving himself to death. During this phase, I recalled that one reason for placing him in the children's home was his mother's mastitis. When I referred to the calamities this elicited, he sighed resignedly that it all is beyond language and proceeded: 'If only the Dorian Gray in me would soon emerge.' Martin was hoping that his inner destructiveness would finally find metaphorical expression in the transference. After realising his precarious somatic condition, he understood that his ego did not function normally.

Martin's miseries evoked castration in my mind. Therefore, I asked him about his present sexual interests. Not surprisingly, he said he had lately thought about the possibility of hormonal medication. Then he recalled a dream: 'I was in a cellar with a rifle in my hands. I admired the weapon that I had just purchased. There was a bed nearby and a lamp that was not on. I was talking with somebody. Then I heard my aunt's voice and hid the rifle under the carpet. I heard her say that there was nobody there.' Martin's associations to the rifle led him first to thoughts of suicide but then to masturbation in his puberty. The carpet represented the bedcover for him and the repression of his phallic interest, which was lifted by my confrontation, allowing his sexual interest to become conscious.

From then on, Martin's regression to his early psychic trauma progressively gave way to an intrapsychic conflict in the transference. Although the calamities of the first year of life still repeated themselves in the analysis, the Oedipal constellation remained in the foreground. Martin's psychosexual identification was, as I have mentioned, predominantly feminine, and his Oedipus complex inverted. The lack of a father had signified bottomless shame. He told me that at the age of two to three years, he had imagined that his mother and her younger sister were a married couple devoid of a penis. On the other hand, he had believed that his aunt could provide him with a penis. In fact, his castration anxiety was also predominantly feminine. After dealing with this topic, he was ready to outline his situation from a new perspective: he had imagined the female genital as an inverted penis and an abyss in which he felt he would drown. In this context, he recalled his inability to learn to swim and wondered why he allowed himself to sink without moving forward. Martin's explanation was that his aggression was also inverted, which reminds us of Gaddini's (1972) idea that it is aggression that ultimately brings the libido toward the objects in the outside world. During the following weeks, his phallic interests became more explicit.

Two months later, Martin was rudely denied entry to a restaurant to meet his wife. In recounting this embarrassing incident, he recalled his mother's cerebral insult half a year earlier, the painful meaning of which he had completely denied at the time. In this period, however, he tearfully realised that his mother had been in mortal danger. At the following session, his vitality had returned as well as his genuine interest in foreign languages. He contemplated some words in Greek – for example, the word *infant*, which denotes one who doesn't speak. Then the word 're-finding' occurred to him and furthered the re-finding of his mother. Martin had always used only diminutives when speaking of his mother. Not until then had he been able to realise the profound emotional meaning of the word 'mother'. He told me that while looking at his wife's breasts the day before, he had touched them and understood that in his native language the verbs 'to grasp' and 'to comprehend' as well as the nouns 'hand' and 'concept' derive from the infant's perceiving and touching his mother's breast.

In short, the traumatised infant in Martin began to recover. Although a bizarre fragmentation of language occurred in the later phases of his analysis, this was hardly perceptible. On the contrary, his associations had the quality of a playful re-discovery of the primary object in the transference, which soon led to another important subject: the aggravation of his drive-instinctual dangers. In his adolescence, he had cut a tendon in his hand. requiring surgical treatment. He now associated this injury with the fear of castration. In referring to our recent linguistic discussion, he said, relieved: 'I have two witnesses to my being a man. Surely you know that the word *testis* in Latin denotes a witness.' An additional association was linked with his feminine wishes and with me 'as a demon behind his back'.

During the third year of analysis Martin purchased an apartment. The agreement was revoked because the sellers committed fraud, though Martin did not take legal action. What seemed to be at stake was more than the repayment of money: the restoration of Martin's rights on a more fundamental level was at issue. Unconsciously, he treated the sellers like parents who had betrayed his vital interests. In the analysis, he was furious with them, and with me for not preventing him from entering into an abortive transaction.

Half a year later Martin's psychic coherence was again severely shaken and his language began to fragment. Instead of displaying the genuine interest he had taken in words, as described above, he now fabricated random etymological connections. He also imagined that Christianity was in danger and that illegitimate sons would be rising to save the world. When I confronted him with the fact that he was replacing the real world with a delusional one, where he was great and powerful instead of feeling small and helpless, he linked the legal proceedings with his sexual fears. The previous night he had woken up with the strong feeling that someone was entering his room. After

I connected his fear with my physical proximity in the analytic setting, Martin recovered his psychic integrity in a few days. Before his psychotic regression he had boasted in his mind about raping me.

From then on, Martin felt free to speak about his anal fantasies and delusional thoughts in the analytical situation. During the following weeks, we understood that an archaic superego conflict aggravated by his legal proceedings had elicited his psychotic fragmentation. He had also imagined that those who literally believe in the Bible would murder him because he had discovered his parents' secret: his mother's bad reputation and his father's avoidance of responsibility. Unconsciously he had filed a lawsuit against the parents in his primal scene.

Although he still had grandiose sadomasochistic fantasies, the focus of the analysis was continually moving towards framing the Oedipus complex. A decisive step forward occurred when Martin grasped towards the end of the fourth year a primal scene fantasy in the transference and was able to reconstruct his parents' love relationship in his mind. Both the positive and negative Oedipal constellations became reconstructed. He imagined inheriting my house if I should happen to die and taking my place as the analyst and also as husband of my wife. However, he was also afraid that I would kill him for these wishes or that I could never accept a feminine man like him as my son.

As so often, the pendulum of the analytic process swung again towards Martin's early trauma, which finally became bound to its original context in the transference: 'It occurred to me yesterday as if there were openings where my wife's breasts should be and serpents in them with gaping mouths. I was shooting them...' I said that his mother's breasts were denied him as a child and that therefore he projected his hunger in the shape of snakes into the empty openings. In the following session, he imagined being a baby at my wife's breast and my looking at him beside her: 'If only my father had visited my mother in the maternity ward.' Then the image of my face occurred to him and he continued: 'My penile sensations have left room for feelings of the heart that have been too painful until now. A cut penis and a cut umbilical cord belong together.... The father also belongs to these fantasies. The touch of the heart comes through you. It is impossible to reach this depth alone.'

Consonant with Freud's (1926) idea of primal castration, Martin dealt with his traumatic separation from his early mother in terms of castration. Only after my interpretation of his oral rage was he able to configure in the transference the stage of Oedipal triangulation.

The image of my face, which occurred to him, reflected the recovery of his primary identification, signifying not only the discovery of the absent father but also genuine feelings and bodily sensations on the metaphorical level (Salonen, 2006).

Toward the end of this session, we were confronted with the full intensity of his hatred for his mother, which had not found outlet in the absence of his father. Martin proceeded: 'I am now facing with killing both of them, or perhaps someone will kill me, an honest man.' At the same time, he felt greatly relieved and exclaimed: 'You are the killer! You know that *paranóos* means 'beside the mind'. It's a thought beside my mind that persecutes me.' When he later returned to his dissociated and projected ideas of killing his mother, he compared this crime with another, namely the theft of his father's penis. He was, finally, dealing with the *basic crime*s of incest, parricide, and castration (Tuovinen, 1973) at the metaphorical level in the transference. His archaic drive-instinctual urges elicited by the primal scene no longer presented themselves as mere deeds. They had now found psychic representation as drive-instinctual wishes.

From then on, Martin was able to extricate himself from his sadomasochistic involvements, and the atmosphere of the sessions lightened. He expressed this change as follows: 'I have arrived. I am in touch with what we once referred to as the primally good.' He felt liberated from something oppressive, reminding him of his first summer holidays at the beginning of his analysis: 'I knew at that time that somewhere in the distance there was someone who cared. I never saw my father. I felt like a lost son.' One can hardly find a more convincing witness of the father's role in the constitution of the mind, as well as in an individual's psychic survival.

After four and half years of analysis, Martin considered the possibility of concluding our work, which we did a half a year later. Martin had been re-watching the movie *The Picture of Dorian Gray*, without any longer identifying with the principal character: 'I saw on the film a frightened human being. I asked myself how all of this could have happened to me. Now, I see that the Evil is equivalent to the experience of being abandoned, being a nonentity.' Referring to his grandiose fantasies, he wondered how difficult it was to accept one's non-heroic heritage. It became evident to Martin that Dorian Gray's picture represented the vindictive hero of his primal scene, born out of his fantasy of forbidden anal intercourse between his parents.

After these remarkable discoveries, Martin felt for a brief period whole: 'Yesterday, I had penile sensations and warm feelings in my heart. That is where they belong, not only in my lower body and genitals. They should also find a place in my heart. I feel like sitting on your belly and searching your face as my little daughter does with me.' This is what I understand by primary identification configuring a frame of reference for the psychic representation of elementary drive phenomena.

Four months before the end of his analysis, Martin's ambivalence towards his psychic integration again became accentuated, and his grandiose ideas reappeared. While dealing with his triumphant Oedipal fantasies, he reported a negative hallucination. After leaving the previous session a white patch had appeared in his field of vision, which he associated to his absent father. He said the same phenomenon had also taken place two years earlier, which at that time was linked to his mother. In reaching for a tomato on the table to cut it, the tomato disappeared from his field of vision. Reporting this incident, he associated it with a nipple: 'The tomato was like a big nipple. There was only one of them like my mother's breast. Her other nipple had disappeared after a surgical operation.' Thus, the negative hallucination became associated with Martin's split-off oral aggression and rage, having been projected into his mother's damaged breast witnessing the infant's primal phantasies: that is, the idea of primal castration.

One month before concluding his analysis, Martin was ready to meet his father in person for the first time. He thought he was finally going to encounter reality. After this remarkable event, he felt bodily recovered: 'Finally, I feel my body as my own, I feel my skin . . . a wish of being caressed by a woman or by you – ultimately – by my father. I could never be proud at my mother's breast; I was drowning in her. What I felt was most important was to see my father's eyes.'

In this context, it is worth remembering that Freud (1923) connected primary identification with object finding, especially finding the father. Seeing his father's eyes signified for Martin a frame of reference in which he could recognise himself as a human being akin to his father and no longer as a nonentity.

Two weeks before leaving, he compared himself with the infant Oedipus whose mother told a servant to forsake King Laios's son: 'That is why my skin is so sensitive, and it also explains the painful stimulation in my genitals.' Martin's infantile trauma had become bound to a major metaphorical narrative in terms of drive-instinctual dangers. Every break in the analysis had signified abandonment, castration and the loss of love, akin to the infant Oedipus in the desert, his feet maimed.

In the final session, Martin was embarrassed about his strong emotions: 'Not until seeing my father was I able to understand how much I missed you during the early holiday breaks. At first, I missed analysis only, but then you as an individual, and another man. It's dawning on me how those children feel who have a real family. I was somewhere in between, a child of two lonely individuals.'

The second scene

Fifteen years later, Martin contacted me after he experienced a series of painful misfortunes. His wife had left him, and his new relationship was also in danger. All the members of his extended childhood family had died. After retiring on account of his somatic illness, he felt like a failure. However, the main reason he contacted me was to talk about his father, who had died three years after his analysis had ended, just before he had officially acknowledged his paternity. Martin held me responsible for his difficulties and therefore liable to pay damages. Underlying this claim was an unconscious constellation that became the subject of our work during the following five years of meeting once to twice a week.

What had intrigued me after concluding Martin's analysis was his anguish at knowing the secret of his parents' love life, as if it were associated with a deadly danger. There was some intimation it was linked, in his mind, to the vindictive father of his primal scene. At that time Martin seemed to arm himself with the weapons of psychoanalysis to conquer his mighty rivals in the external world. Instead of victories, he felt he had suffered defeat after defeat. No wonder then that he became disappointed with his analyst, who begun to represent the ultimate cause of his calamities.

Another remarkable event was his father's early death, the impact of which exceeded Martin's capacity to mourn and which lead to a paralysing regression and exacerbation of his paranoid hostility, directed toward his former supervisor and me. He held me responsible for not inducing him to meet his father at the beginning of analysis – as if I had been able to foresee his father's future death. Another accusation was more serious. It was that psychoanalysis had been an incorrect method in his case, a question that I had often asked myself during his treatment.

In any case, when Martin returned, I became the object of his paranoid hostility and murderous thoughts, which remained contained within the framework of the analytic relationship. My primary task was to maintain my analytic stance in the face of his hostility and my feelings of guilt as a result of my possibly having damaged Martin's psychic health. My task was to survive as his analyst (Winnicott, 1969, 1971). It took time for me to understand that I represented a combined primary object in the transference, that is, his parents, whom Martin held responsible for neglecting his vital interests. Only after being confronted with my feeling of helplessness did I come to understand his mother's difficult position: her bewildering ambivalence and her feelings of shame and guilt in facing alone the vital needs of her baby.

Martin's accusation that I had not induced him to meet his father exactly corresponded with his criticism of his mother. It was even more painful for me to hear Martin's reproach that I had applied the wrong treatment in his case; here too, my feelings appeared to correspond to his mother's feelings of helplessness and guilt at the beginning of her son's life. However, I had offered him an opportunity to work through his infantile trauma in the analytic setting. This realisation on my part decisively alleviated my countertransference problems and helped me remain open to the possibility that I had made serious errors within the framework of Martin's treatment. Toward the end of our work, Martin returned to these points: 'You have never betrayed me, and never denied the possibility of your having made mistakes.' He understood that his mother's profound helplessness had not only prevented him from claiming his parental legacy but also that his mother most likely would not have been able to admit to her mistakes nor survive Martin's aggression without the support of her child's father.

Contained in the analytical setting, Martin's rage receded, and he began to understand that his father's death was outside of our control, at the same time recognising his mother lacked the capacity to cope with his quest for paternal love. The clarification of these two aspects of the transference restored Martin's confidence in me, and he was able to continue his analytic work. For the first time, he accepted his divorce as a sad loss without accusing his wife of any wrongdoing. He was also able to regard his early retirement as a necessity. However, this progress was not possible without an additional repetition of his early trauma in the transference, this time in the form of a deep depression, albeit without psychic fragmentation. In his despair, Martin lost his appetite and began to smoke heavily, creating a serious health risk. Again, his lifeless complexion evoked an image of castration in my mind. In this connection, he finally recalled a major conflict with his supervisor, discussed at the beginning of his analysis. This incident had taken place two years before our first meeting.

Without anticipating the serious consequences, Martin had joined an attempt by his colleagues to oust their supervisor from an important project. Unable at that time to deal with his unconscious patricidal wishes and the attendant guilt, he succumbed to depression. When the offended supervisor also withdrew all his support from his protégée, Martin was forced to face an ancient calamity, the loss of the father's love, which lead to the collapse of his drive-instinctual sublimations, on which his psychic integration was based.

After a year and a half my preliminary impression that knowing the secrecy of his parents' love life signified a deadly danger for Martin was confirmed. When he was grieving for his miseries, I asked whether this state of mind possibly reflected a delusion about his own person. Conforming to my interpretation, Martin told me he believed that I had factually castrated him as a result of the psychoanalytic treatment, which of course even further elucidated his claims for compensation. In discussing the Latin word *deludere*, Martin finally realised that he had deceived his senses into believing himself to be castrated.

For Martin, castration was not merely a potential danger to his manliness, but a fact inferred from his strange bodily sensations. We can regard his delusion as a derivative of the traumatic separation from the early fusion with his mother; something more specific was needed, however, to understand the full intensity of Martin's agony. This was the presence of the primal father as castrator in the transference.

During the following three years, we met less frequently. When the decision to conclude our work had already been made, Martin faced an additional hardship: he suffered a heart attack, which was treated by angioplasty. This confrontation with the danger of actual death led to a profound change in his life. Unable to deny the genuine love shown by his children and grandchildren in visiting him at the hospital, Martin discovered his real significance as a father and grandfather. When we met for the last time, a few weeks after his heart attack, Martin seemed to be calm and composed. In looking back at our work, he characterised the initial five-year period of his analysis as a repetition of his desperate search for a childhood in his relationship with me, then the subsequent period as a process of becoming conscious of the meanings of this search. In this session Martin reflected upon human vulnerability in general. Full of sorrow, he remembered his war-disabled psychotic uncle, then his son who had suffered a traffic accident as a little child. He said that every generation has scars of its own and that the world does not seem to be changing for the better. Coming back to his son's accident, he said it was not the driver's fault, but that on the contrary he did everything in his power to prevent the child from bleeding to death. Martin was also talking about himself and his analyst. He was sad but no longer depressed.

In the end Martin succeeded in integrating his loss within the framework of hope discovered not only through his analysis but also through his children and grandchildren: that is, his paternity. I think that his search for the absent father in the transference had not been in vain. Although psychoanalysis could not recompense his loss, it enabled Martin to remove the unconscious obstacles to finding his biological father, and also to re-find the absent father of the primal scene in a human shape, signifying primary identification.

An additional remark on primary identification

André Green's (1986, 2004) starting point for understanding the origins of the infant's psychic development was the parents' sexual relationship. He did not derive this process exclusively from the mother, but underlined the significance of the father as the mother's lover from the beginning of life. In Green's analysis, the primal scene is linked to the absent father, since the only present object for the infant is the object of fusion with the mother. Therefore, the primal scene remains outside the infant's comprehension and is a traumatic experience. Thus, the primal scene does not in the first place manifest an exposure to the parents' sexual act, but rather an encounter with the awakening drive in the infant himself. What becomes perceived forms a lifelong challenge in respect of psychic representation of elementary drive phenomena. At this point, primary identification re-enters our discussion.

I shall return to Martin's nameless horror in watching the movie *The Picture of Dorian Gray*, which evoked his primal scene. In re-watching the same movie after five years of analysis, he was able to disengage himself from his horror. Showing compassion and clear insight, Martin told me that he had recognised this time a frightened human being. In the psychoanalytic setting, he had found a human face for his horror as well as the capacity to deal metaphorically with his humiliation and narcissistic rage in the transference.

Joyce McDougall (1980) proposed that the enigma of sexual desire lies in the mother's missing penis and the child's preconscious knowledge that only the father's penis can ever complete her genital. In meeting his father for the first time, Martin recognised the absent father in a human shape rather than the horrifying figure of his primal scene.

Martin's swimming lessons did not merely indicate a biological urge to escape from drowning in the water, but also his preconscious wish for psychic survival in the transference. This wish was discernible throughout his analysis as a hidden *cantus firmus*, which Birgitta Ejve (2002) related to variations of human sexuality in the analytic relationship, carrying vital meanings and continuity of psychic experience throughout an individual's life.

Note

1 The paper was originally published in *Scand. Psychoanal. Rev.*, 34: 85–94 (2011). Copyright© The Psychoanalytic Societies of Denmark, Finland, Norway, and Sweden, reprinted by permission of Taylor & Francis Ltd, www.tandfonline.com on behalf of The Psychoanalytic Societies of Denmark, Finland, Norway, and Sweden.

References

Chasseguet-Smirgel, J. (1988). From the archaic matrix of the Oedipus complex to the fully developed Oedipus complex: The theoretical perspective in relation to clinical experience and technique. *Psychoanal. Q.*, 57: 505–527.

Ejve, B. (2002). The presence of sexuality as *cantus firmus* with variations: thoughts about transference and countertransference. *Scand. Psychoanal. Rev.*, 25: 56–61.

Freud, S. (1923). The ego and the id. In *The Standard Edition of the Complete Psychological Works of Sigmund Freud*, Volume XIX, pp. 1–66.

Freud, S. (1926). Inhibitions, symptoms and anxiety. In *The Standard Edition of the Complete Psychological Works of Sigmund Freud*, Volume XX, pp. 75–176.

Gaddini, E. (1972). Aggression and the pleasure principle: Towards a psychoanalytic theory of aggression. In *A Psychoanalytic Theory of Infantile Experience*. Limentani, A. (editor). London, New York: Tavistock/Routledge, 1992, pp. 35–45.

Green, A. (1986). The dead mother. In *On Private Madness*. London: The Hogarth Press and the Institute of Psychoanalysis, pp. 158–161. Reference to *Narcissisme vie: Narcissisme de mort*. Paris: Minuit, 1983.

Green, A. (2004). Thirdness and psychoanalytic concepts. *Psychoanal. Q.*, 73: 99–135.

McDougall, J. (1980). *Plea for a Measure of Abnormality*. New York: Int. Univ. Press, p. 74.

Rangell, L. (1954). The psychology of poise – with a special elaboration on the psychic significance of the snout or perioral region. *Int. J. Psycho-Anal.*, 35: 313–332.

Salonen, S. (2006). The body and the sense of reality. In *Beyond the Mind-Body Dualism: Psychoanalysis and the Human Body*. Zacharacopoulou, E. (editor). Amsterdam: Elsevier International Congress Series #1286, pp. 33–40.

Tuovinen, M. (1973). *Crime as an Attempt at Intrapsychic Adaptation*. Acta Universitatis Ouluensis, Series D, Medica no. 2, Psychiatrica no 1. Oulu: University of Oulu.

Wilde, O. (1891). *The Picture of Dorian Gray*. The Finnish translation: *Dorian Grayn muotokuva*. Porvoo: Werner Söderström Osakeyhtiö, 1963.

Winnicott, D. W. (1969). The use of an object. *Int. J. Psychoanal.*, 50: 711–716.

Winnicott, D. W. (1971). The use of an object and relating through identifications. In *Playing and Reality*. Harmondsworth: Penguin Books, pp. 101–111.

12

ON THE METAPSYCHOLOGY OF PSYCHIC SURVIVAL

At the beginning of her session, my analysand, a woman in her forties, experienced the smells in my office as a pleasurable message from all my previous analysands. As she reclined on the couch, she imagined lying on the top of them, as if they were forming a pile under her: 'They all are here', she said. After a while, she proceeded: 'A pile of firewood occurs to me. While playing there as a child, I once crawled into a hollow space. I was terribly scared of the pile collapsing on me. It is just this threatening atmosphere that writers attempt to translate into words in their struggle against the powers of oblivion and destruction; I mean the reality of time.'

Her last sentence touched me and I made a note for myself without at that time grasping its significance. Only now, over twenty years later, I can understand that she was talking about the psychoanalytic setting representing the metaphorical space within which the unconscious psychic processes receive meanings as well as about the collapse of this space when confronted with the temporal limitation on individual life. This piece of analytic work epitomises the crux of my theoretical approach: the integration of traumatic helplessness into the sphere of psychic representation, forming a counterpoint to escalating destruction and despair. The particular quality of hope characterising the psychoanalytic setting is based on an opportunity of this integration.

The conceptual space of psychoanalysis

We may think metapsychology is removed from the ordinary psychoanalytic experience and clinical work. It is not immediately apparent to us that it explores vital forces and meanings on which an individual's psychic existence depends. Perhaps we only recognise these phenomena as distressing symptoms or a paralysing horror at those moments when our life feels seriously threatened. Despite the pervasive presence of these elements, we can grasp them only through theoretical abstractions. In short, we are dealing here with unconscious psychic reality, the ultimate knowledge of which Freud thought to be as removed a goal as the grasping of physical reality. With his drive theory Freud delineated a conceptual space, indicating how to approach this reality from different points of view. Psychoanalytic thinking represents the analyst's creative activity within this conceptual space. Metapsychology, for its part, constitutes an atlas for the analyst, a multidimensional map, upon which psychoanalytic observations are projected for shared understanding (Salonen, 2004).

Customarily we think that the dimension of time does not exist in the unconscious, that there are no contradictions or limitations, no death either. Unconscious psychic reality is thought to be a servant to the almighty pleasure principle. Insofar as we follow Freud's first topographical model, we have no reason to doubt this definition. However, the problem becomes more complicated when we consider Freud's structural theory, also called his second topography. What holds true of the unconscious in the first topography applies only to the id, but not to the unconscious part of the ego. Thus, we find ourselves here on a frontier where the primary process will transform into the secondary process after being associated with words to create preconscious meanings. More time is needed, however, before these meanings may attain consciousness. In the episode mentioned above, it took decades for my part. This is what Freud (1898, 1918) meant by *Nachträglichkeit*, i.e., deferred action.

In Freud's structural model, becoming conscious is something more than grasping a meaning from within. It signifies shaping the realities of life from a new perspective in association with an earlier preconscious understanding that becomes manifest only retroactively in the course of individual life. In this model, consciousness signifies a structured understanding within a metaphorical space, extending into the temporal dimension. Hans Loewald (1962) first posited that psychic structures would be temporal. I will return to this question toward the end of this chapter, after first discussing the great turning point in Freud's metapsychological thinking between 1917 and the early 1920s.

Integration of fundamental ambivalence

Freud's *Mourning and Melancholia* (1917) marked a turning point in his theoretical thinking, comprising the final essay in a series of his metapsychological papers. It was based on 20 years of clinical experience and an in-depth analysis of drive-instinctual wishes and the pleasure principle regulating psychic processes. Initially, his plan was to publish seven other papers in this series; this plan was never realised. Instead, he subsequently published *Beyond the Pleasure Principle*, which subjected the foundations of psychoanalytic drive theory to a critical reappraisal (Freud, 1920).

In *Mourning and Melancholia*, Freud compared mourning with the pathological affect state found in melancholia. Despite many apparent similarities, these affect states differ radically from each other. Mourning is the expression of a painful bereavement of a cherished object, the loss of which is coupled with the feeling that the world has been divested of all meaning. Nevertheless, mourning is a solid affect state, within which the gradual working through of the painful loss will be possible. In time, this leads to the psychic integration of an individual's ambivalence towards the lost object, and finally to new possibilities of delight and gratitude for all that was experienced along with the deceased person. Thus, the living memory of the lost object is part and parcel of this integration. Melancholia, by contrast, is a collapsed affect state and signifies a catastrophic loss of self-esteem. In this case, there is no integration of ambivalence but only interludes in a devastating intrapsychic process, which may include an actual danger of self-destruction.

Freud had difficulties understanding why anyone would want to commit suicide in the light of psychoanalytic knowledge revealing the immense quantity of primary narcissistic interest through which an individual becomes originally attached to life and which becomes released in extreme psychic trauma. Freud thought that suicide becomes understandable only when the destruction directed against the self is linked to a painful narcissistic injury concealing a narcissistic relationship with the primary object. As a result of inward aggression, this fragile object tie becomes severed, causing the ego to regress to the level of primary identification. After this, cannibalistic oral aggression will be discharged freely until it consumes the self without any structural transformation. As a result, psychotic depression tends to repeat itself unchanged.

Freud thought that the ambivalence inherent in melancholia is connected to an injured primary narcissism, resulting in extreme psychic pain or agony, in German *Schmerz*. Like physical pain, it attracts all libidinal interest available, ultimately leading to a paralysis of the ego. In this connection, it may be relevant to speak of an individual's ambivalence towards life itself, or fundamental ambivalence, which applies not only to psychotic depression but also to serious psychosomatic illnesses that also may represent a mortal danger. The ambivalence linked with mourning is possible to integrate through the process of working through it. According to Freud, the mourner ultimately has a choice between renouncing his lost libidinal object or his psychic vitality. By contrast, the melancholic individual does not have such freedom of choice after the collapse of his psychic functioning.

In *Beyond the Pleasure Principle* (1920), Freud transferred the discussion of ambivalence and psychic survival to another conceptual level, while at the same time finding an answer to the question intriguing him, namely the problem of the monistic versus the dualistic nature of psychoanalytic drive theory. His new conceptualisation was dualistic: the life drive and the death drive. Freud's starting point was his observations of repetition compulsion related to psychic trauma, which he felt contradicted his libido theory clearly formulated in his metapsychological papers. He was attempting to understand why painful, traumatic experiences continue to repeat themselves, despite being devoid of any elements of pleasure and consolation.

Freud embarked on an explanation related to biological instincts which no longer were derived from the body and its vital functions, as previously thought, but were seen as characteristic of organic life in general. Through biological speculations, he arrived at the idea that repetition compulsion exemplifies the conservative nature of drives in the sense that their ultimate goal is to return all life to its origins, namely, an inorganic state. Although *Eros* creates new combinations of life, this only secures for an individual and species its own circuitous way to death. Thus, the life drive too proved to be in Freud's metapsychological thinking the Myrmidon of death, creating vital tensions only to gradually expire: to *abgelebt werden*.

Although Freud initially believed his concepts were original, he acknowledged toward the end of his life his debt of gratitude to philosophers who influenced his thinking. In his *Analysis Terminable and Interminable* (1937), he returned to this question after discovering the thoughts of the Pre-Socratic philosopher Empedocles, who came astonishingly close to his dualistic drive theory, although Empedocles' philosophy applied to nature as a whole and not only organic life. Freud could not remember having consciously thought about this connection, although he considered cryptomnesia to be possible (Freud, 1937). Freud thus became aware that his metapsychological thinking was influenced by his *Weltanschauung*. Having initially conceived his new ideas more tentatively, uncertain of their validity, he wrote that with time these ideas had exerted such a hold on him that he was no longer able to think in another way.

Freud's personal physician, Max Schur, analysed his patient's unconscious motives for adopting the concept of the death drive in his book *Freud Living and Dying* (1972), concluding that the main motive was Freud's ambivalence in facing his death. This supports my hypothesis that Freud's work *Mourning and Melancholia* (1917), in which the ambivalence constitutes a central theme, forms a turning point in his metapsychological thinking. The elderly Freud's dilemma was how to face one's death without having recourse to religious or metaphysical solutions outside psychoanalysis. Schur writes:

> Therefore, the formulation of the death-instinct concept – paradoxical as this may seem – may not only have steeled Freud for the sixteen years' ordeal of his cancer, but prepared him for his belief in the supremacy of the ego, of the intellect, of Logos, the only force with which he could face Ananke. It paved the way for the Future of an Illusion and for the formulation of a "scientific Weltanschauung".
>
> (1972, p. 332)

Freud's dualistic drive theory was rooted in his belief that death forms the ultimate aim of instinctual drives and that life respectively can be understood as a circuitous path towards this destination. When Freud returned to this theme in his last works, he thought his approach perhaps reflected a Schopenhauerian pessimism, and suspected that he had underestimated the importance of *Eros*. In any case, psychoanalytic thinking helped him not only to resign himself to *Necessity* but also to grasp his fundamental ambivalence by linking it with the general principles of organic life. Thus, Freud had found a drive-instinctual explanation for an individual's entire lifespan within the confines of which the unconscious psychic processes receive preconscious meanings. One of the great sources of meaning in Freud's life was, of course, psychoanalysis itself, which he knew would survive him and preserve his memory for future generations. All this indicated the integration of his ambivalence as well as the sublimation of his primary narcissism at the level of shared cultural values, consonant with his ego-ideal.

Conflicting observations

In the following discussion, I will focus on the observations in conflict with the pleasure principle, one of them being the analysand's enigmatic tendency to undermine his or her therapeutic achievements, which Freud related it to the death drive. While in *Mourning and Melancholia* (1917) he had difficulties in understanding how someone could commit suicide, despite one's primary narcissistic interest in life, he now coupled primary narcissism with an analogous destructive drive potential: primary masochism. This innovation was introduced in a short albeit trenchant essay *The Economic Problem of Masochism* (Freud, 1924), which Eugenio Gaddini characterised as the most important paper ever written on the internal distribution of aggression in the human organism (Gaddini, 1972).

Freud's starting point was the agonising pain to which an individual may become addicted. He wrote this article at a critical period of his life, when his personal mishaps and miseries seem to have been almost overwhelming. In 1920, his daughter Sophie had died of the Spanish flu, and three years later her little son Heinerle also died after a short bout of tuberculosis. Half a year after this Freud was diagnosed with cancer, and the painful treatment procedures, which lasted sixteen years, were initiated. According to Ernst Jones (1957, pp. 94–106), the death of his grandson left him deeply depressed to the point where he felt incapable of ever surviving this misfortune. This spate of death and dying, which surely reminded him of the death of his younger brother Julius, when Sigmund was less than two years old, threatened his sense of integrity.

Betty Joseph (1982) observed that many patients who become addicted to living close to death have suffered some painful physical condition in their early infancy. Although paradoxical, the erotised suffering may form an ultimate bridgehead for the helpless ego in its struggle against internal destruction. If interwoven into the ego-ideal, primary masochism becomes the source of moral masochism, where internal destruction has been subjected to the dominance of the pleasure principle without forming an imminent threat to individual survival, as in the case of primary masochism. In this sense, moral masochism can be seen as a developmental achievement, where primary masochism is bound to the psychic structure (De M'Uzan, 1973).

Hitherto, I have referred to destructive drive phenomena instead of the death drive. I have thus kept a certain distance from Freud's natural philosophy. Instead of incorporating death into the ultimate explanatory principles of psychoanalysis, I have approached extreme psychic trauma from the viewpoint of the vulnerable ego. However, this divergence of views may not be insurmountable. It depends on two different conceptualisations of primary identification. As presented above, in *Mourning and Melancholia* (1917) Freud approached this notion in oral-incorporative terms, in line with Abraham, which also applies to his second drive theory. Three years later, in *The Ego and the Id*, Freud (1923) connected primary identification with object finding and the ego-ideal, which forms the starting point of my structural thinking. It is likely that the same dichotomy also divides the psychoanalytic tradition at large.

In my analysis, the notion of destructive drive phenomena refers to drive elements that present themselves before the rudimentary ego as destructive deeds, devoid of psychic representation, analogous to Bion's (1970) beta-elements. This is consonant with Freud's view in *Totem and Taboo* (1913), where he maintained that thought is preceded in the unconscious by deeds expressing the ultimate aims of the instinctual drive.

Two illustrations

I would like to elucidate my metapsychological starting points with two brief examples, the first of which deals with the birth of tiger cubs in a TV documentary, and the second with a recollection from the early stages of my medical studies many decades ago. These examples illustrate both ends of the human lifespan from a drive-economic point of view.

The TV documentary followed the daily life of a tiger family, showing how a young tigress gave birth to two cubs at an hour's interval. The first-born crawled energetically towards the mother's nipple. After the cub attained its goal, the mother licked it, then took care of it with all her instinctive tenderness. The other cub appeared weak and lethargic. The mother didn't show any interest in it. Wearily, the cub dragged itself towards the mother's nipple, which seemed to be hopelessly far away. After an hour of desperate wandering, it finally reached its destination with its last reserve of strength. Then the mother licked this cub too and accepted it as her own. Little by little the cub recovered to begin the life of its species.

This episode suggests a biological urge for survival which inherently harbours a component of aggression. The efforts of the tiger cubs to reach the mother's nipple manifested this urge, which also forms an essential precondition of human psychic survival. The etymology of the word 'aggression' derives from the Latin words *aggredi*, to attack, and *ag-gradi*, to step toward. Although we cannot draw a direct parallel between the ethological imprinting of the tiger mother and her cubs and the primary identification of the human infant, the analogy is clear.

Moreover, human psychic survival is based on the infant's primary narcissistic *interest* in achieving this goal. In the case of radical psychic trauma, this vital resource may be exhausted, leading ultimately to a state of despair, an inner object of fusion with the destroyed primary object. This kind of discharge of crude aggression also explains the paralysing feelings of guilt haunting survivors of extreme psychic trauma.

Characteristic of radical psychic trauma is a recurring sound or vision impossible to locate in space and time. The rudimentary ego is exposed to strange psychic elements felt to be cosmic in nature. We can approach this mode of experience in children's night terrors when they wander astray until hearing their mother's voice returns them to familiar reality (Stern, 1988). The child getting up and wandering or rushing from his bed towards his parents is analogous to the tiger cubs crawling towards their mother's nipple, a behaviour pattern suggesting an instinctive search for the primary object, which acquires meaning only at its destination. This is consonant with Renata Gaddini's (2002, 2003) observations about the first precursors of the transitional object. In analogy to Stella Polaris in high seas navigation, the inborn image of the mother's nipple allows metaphorical navigation throughout an individual's life.

My second example concerns a male patient in his sixties who died after an operation. His vital functions already failing, he sank into a delirious state, and his speech was difficult to follow, but before he died, he said quite clearly: 'Perhaps it's time to reverse towards death.' Although his physical and psychic resources were not sufficient to sustain full consciousness, his rudimentary ego seemed aware of the actual situation. The reversal towards death did not indicate in the first place a temporal regression, but an affirmative renunciation of his primary narcissistic interest in life in facing its ultimate limitation. Thus, imminent death does not inevitably signify destruction; it may also represent an opportunity for a final integration. Paul Ricoeur (2009) approached this ultimate limit of individual life in his posthumous *Living Up to Death*, comprising the same idea.

The destructive compulsion to repeat past calamities is related to early psychic trauma. Even in the case when the human infant has attained its primary goal and survived, it may for some reason or other become susceptible later to overwhelming traumatic helplessness. As a result of lack of capacity for psychic representation, it then remains at the mercy of destructive forces. Regarding the rudimentary ego, this signifies a threat of annihilation. Only after these destructive elements are bound to an evolving psychic structure can available resources of aggression be harnessed by the ego to carry out its generative task on the advanced level of psychic organisation.

Freud (1924) was not satisfied with his attempts to integrate the pleasure principle into his new theory of the life drive and the death drive. He considered the possibility that some unknown qualitative factor might still be involved, which could be rhythmic or temporal. However, in the end he concluded that these two principles of psychic regulation functioned separately, and that the pleasure principle can be regarded as the 'guardian of our life.' Subsequently, he returned to this problem in his posthumous *Outline of Psychoanalysis:*

> The id, cut off from the external world, has a world of perception of its own. It detects with extraordinary acuteness certain changes in its interior, especially oscillations in the tension of its instinctual needs, and these changes become conscious as feelings in the pleasure-unpleasure series. It is hard to say, to be sure, by what means and with the help of what sensory terminal organs these perceptions come about. But it is an established fact that self-perceptions – coenaesthetic feelings and feelings of pleasure-unpleasure – govern the passage of events in the id with despotic force. The id obeys the inexorable pleasure principle. But not the id alone. It seems that the activity of the other psychical agencies too is able only to modify

the pleasure principle but not to nullify it; and it remains a question of the highest theoretical importance, and one that has not yet been answered, when and how it is ever possible for the pleasure principle to be overcome. The consideration that the pleasure principle demands a reduction, at bottom the extinction perhaps, of the tensions of instinctual needs (that is, Nirvana) leads to the still unassessed relations between the pleasure principle and the two primal forces, Eros and the death instinct.

(Freud, 1940, p. 198)

Before returning to this question, we have to explore the ego from a structural point of view.

The vulnerable ego

In *Beyond the Pleasure Principle* (1920) Freud compared the emerging psychic organisation to a simple biological organism protected by its surface from 'the enormous energies at work in the external world'. According to him psychic trauma was analogous to a breach of this stimulus barrier, and signifies a threat of annihilation to the organism. I think only after becoming confronted with this threat within himself was Freud (1923) able to conceptualise the psychic reality from a new perspective as a functional whole.

Freud's new approach was more than a mere theoretical construct. It signified a new chance of exploring the dramatic conditions of the emerging ego in the midst of psychic elemental forces and configurations in the process of organisation. Metaphorically speaking, where psychic trauma signifies a state of being abandoned outside the sphere of primary identification, this new approach marks a return to regular psychic functioning, no longer signifying the extreme helplessness of the ego but its relative strength, based on integrated psychic functioning and a consolidated signal of anxiety at the ego's disposal.

The integration of the human mind does not of course take place in a vacuum but is a developmental achievement, the starting point of which is the infant's vital dependence on parental care resulting in the development of a psychic faculty, which Freud considered the heir of past object relations, that is, the ego. Consonant with Veikko Tähkä's (1993) metapsychological reflections, we can speak of a child's *functional legacy* from its parents. Moreover, the child's parental legacy consists of integrated memories as containers of the meaningful past, to which we will return at the end of this chapter.

The word 'helplessness', *Hilflosigkeit*, is found only once in Freud's *The Ego and the Id* (1923) and not at all in *The Economic Problem of Masochism* (1924). In *Inhibition, Symptom and Anxiety* (1926) this word is found 26 times. Freud's main interest at this stage seemed to have moved from extreme psychic trauma and destructive drive phenomena to intrapsychic conflict. His understanding of anxiety was also transformed. He no longer considered anxiety as reflecting drive-economic conditions as such, but came to understand it as an affect response and a danger signal. This signal enables the ego to regulate drive economy by summoning the pleasure principle to react to danger, as in the case of imminent psychic trauma, by reinforcing counter-cathexes of primal repression. In this way, the ego can influence with small investments of psychic energy the distribution of drive-economic resources, while at the same time directing them according to the demands of genital reality. Freud commented on this change in his new theoretical approach in *Inhibitions, Symptoms and Anxiety* (Freud, 1926, p. 95):

> At this point, it is relevant to ask how I can reconcile this acknowledgement of the might of the ego with the description of its position which I gave to in *The Ego and the Id*. In that book, I drew a picture of its dependent relationship to the id and to the superego and revealed how powerless and apprehensive it was in regard to both and with what an effort it maintained its show of superiority over them. This view has been widely echoed in psycho-analytic literature. Many writers have laid much stress on the weakness of the ego in relation to the id and of our rational elements in the face of the daemonic forces within us; and they display a strong tendency to make what I have said into a corner-stone of a psychoanalytic Weltanschauung. Yet surely the psycho-analyst, with his knowledge of the way in which repression works, should, of all people, be restrained from adopting such an extreme and one-sided view.
>
> (1926, p. 95)

The structural theory offered a new possibility for conceptualising psychic conflict from the standpoint of the rudimentary ego. After understanding the ego's traumatic helplessness, Freud was able to visualise intrapsychic conflict in the context of vulnerable libidinal wishes and drive-instinctual dangers of separation, castration, and the loss of love. According to Freud, the drive-instinctual dangers become ultimately integrated into psychic functioning as a danger signal. This integration also signifies a structural reorganisation of the ego itself. After achieving Oedipal solutions, an ideal frame of reference and critical faculty is placed at the ego's disposal, allowing for the possibility of an inner dialogue with one's developmental *history* from the viewpoint of intrapsychic conflict. The fact that an individual's fundamental ambivalence in facing one's death becomes drawn into this process of structural transformation implies that psychoanalysis may in some cases prove to be an extremely painful process.

The unconscious foundations of psychic survival

During the psychoanalytic treatment of psychotic and severely traumatised patients, we can observe that the rediscovery of the primary object in the transference may lead to an instant recovery of psychic functioning and revitalisation of affect experience. In the previous chapters, I have connected this observation with Freud's notion of primary identification, which in *Mourning and Melancholia* (1917) was still dealt with as an oral-incorporative phenomenon (Jones, 1955, pp. 367–368). When Freud returned to primary identification in *The Ego and the Id* (1923) he connected it with object finding before ordinary object ties. In his new approach, he related primary identification to the father, although he also suggested both parents may be involved. In any case, Freud associated primary identification in this context with the emergence of the ego-ideal.

Gaddini (1982) described a circular image occurring in children's drawings and the nightmares of adult patients during psychoanalytic treatment, derived from the infant's somatosensory contact with its mother. He maintained that the urge for psychic survival was originally anchored to it. I have linked this configuration to primary identification.

Green (1986) described an analogous psychic formation which he related to the fading of the maternal fusion object. According to Green, this configuration forms a container for the future representational world. This point has helped me understand the fundamental importance of primary identification in creating the capacity for psychic representation. Moreover, in defining the container function from a structural point of view, Green succeeded in building a conceptual bridge between Freud's structural theory and Bion's (1963, 1965) seminal contributions to our understanding of elementary psychic processes.

The early frame for psychic representation cannot be derived solely from the mother. It is related to the metaphorical presence of father; first in the mother's mind and then in the parents' genital relationship into the frame of which the child was born. My focus centres on genital reality as an organising principle of the human mind from birth onwards, the preconscious meanings of which the infant can comprehend only retroactively. Jacqueline Amati Mehler's (2013) recent work on fatherhood and Jean-Claude Stoloff's (2013) studies on the paternal function are remarkable in this area as well as Claudio Eizirik's (2013) profound analysis of the cultural significances of the father from a wider temporal perspective.

The particular position of the father depends on the fact that he represents genital reality not only for the infant's mother but the infant as well. The biological father is the only human being who may acknowledge his paternity and thus confirm the child's separate psychic existence at the level of primal phantasies. Thus, the primary identification signifies the discovery of filiation and, for the father, fatherhood. In short, finding the father signifies a counterpoint to early maternal fusion implying an oral-cannibalistic phantasy of the primal father as epitomised by the myth of Kronos, the Titan god of time, who devoured his children (Eizirik, 2013). Instead of the threat of annihilation, finding the father constitutes the temporal dimension in the infant's mind, implying an anticipation of the future.

From the structural point of view, primary identification frames the ego–ideal which, together with the superego, creates an advanced structure for psychic survival. Since Freud, the ego–ideal has been regarded as a projection of the infant's primary narcissism onto the future. It does not, however, signify unlimited narcissism, but psychic vitality and integrity framed by the genital reality, which Janine Chasseguet-Smirgel (1985) designated almost poetically as the Father-Creator's genital world. Bodily wellbeing and the experience of being alive belong to this category of meaning, as well as human dignity. Only after these meanings are severely endangered can their importance be fully recognised. What is at stake here is the *drive-instinctual foundation of the confidence in life.*

Returning to Freud's creation

In *The Dead Mother* (1986), referred to often in this book, André Green (1986) connected psychic trauma with the mother's depression. In this context, he also mentioned Freud's mother. Sigmund was less than two years old when his younger brother Julius died, when his mother was compelled to face the greatest conceivable loss. We can understand under these conditions the surviving sibling may incorporate this devastating catastrophe into the drive-instinctual foundations of his developing mind without being able to deal with it on a secondary process level. Instead, the catastrophe may be treated as the ideational representative of an instinctual drive (Sandler and Nagera, 1963), perhaps the death drive determining the course of individual life.

From the viewpoint of the maternal fusion object, the despairing mother is not merely absent; her person may embody death and dying. The child is forced to withdraw himself from this experience by resorting to precocious individuation and the activation of intellectual capacities to rescue his vital psychic resources. In Freud's case, this painful dilemma found a creative solution in the psychoanalytic method, which enabled him not only to understand the conflictual nature of human sexuality but also integrate radical psychic trauma into the realm of psychic representation. Thus, not only Freud's father but also his mother can be recognised in his metapsychological thinking.

Freud may have come into contact with Empedocles' philosophy in his youth. Just as my analysand's contemplation of the *traumatic aspect of time* evoked a preconscious response in my mind, Empedocles' ideas may have evoked a similar response in the young student's mind, offering Freud a preconscious idea for configuring his early psychic trauma. However, a structured understanding became possible for Freud only retroactively – half a century later. The central idea of his dualistic drive theory positing that death and destruction inherently belong to organic life was confirmed in his mind not only by the disasters of the war but also by his personal bereavements – as long as they did not destroy his genuine interest in life. Psychoanalysis can therefore be seen not only as an intellectual achievement but also a memorial of Freud's early struggle for psychic survival; and as a clinical method and comprehensive theory, it represents for many an ideal frame of reference for configuring psychic reality and expanding the knowledge of unconscious psychic processes.

The temporal point of view

Freud's dilemma regarding the two different principles of psychic regulation – the pleasure principle and the instincts of life and death – was impossible to solve solely from the drive-economic point of view. The solution can be found on the organised level of psychic functioning in relation to genital reality first represented by the parents for their child. The issue is a lifelong process of structural transformation within an individual's preconscious mind where the pleasure principle gives way to the perceived reality, also involving the painful recognition that one's time is limited.

An individual's lifetime refers to a metaphorical space related to the ego-ideal. In containing the integrated memories of lost objects, the ego-ideal frames the meaningful past. Projected onto the future, it represents hope, forming a container not only for object-libidinal wishes but also a primary narcissistic interest in life, vitalising psychic experience. The recovery of this interest is not possible without the capacity for mourning and sorrow, adumbrating the subtle delight of being alive, that is, the integration of an individual's fundamental ambivalence. From this point of view, psychic survival refers to a process of inner transformation in accordance with genital reality involving a temporal limitation on individual life.

References

Amati Mehler, J. (2013). The vicissitudes of fatherhood. A paper read at the *8th Delphi International Psychoanalytic Symposium*, 21–24 June – Delphi, Greece.

Bion, W. R. (1963). *Elements of Psychoanalysis*. London: William Heinemann Medical Books.

Bion, W. R. (1965). *Transformations*. London: William Heinemann Medical Books.

Bion, W. R. (1970). *Attention and Interpretation*. London: William Heineman Medical Books Ltd.

Chasseguet-Smirgel, J. (1985). *Creativity and Perversion*. London: Free Association Book.

De M'Uzan, M. (1973). A case of masochistic perversion and an outline of a theory. *Int. J. Psychoanal.*, 54: 455–467.

Eizirik, C. L. (2013). The father: Mythology, poetry, psychoanalysis. A paper read at the *8th Delphi International Psychoanalytic Symposium*, 21–24 June – Delphi, Greece.

Freud, S. (1898). Die Sexualität in der Ätiologie der Neurosen. *Gesammelte Werke*, I, 491–516.

Freud, S. (1913). Totem and taboo. In *The Standard Edition of the Complete Psychological Works of Sigmund Freud*, Volume XIII. London: The Hogarth Press and the Institute of Psychoanalysis, p. 161.

Freud, S. (1917). Mourning and melancholia. In *The Standard Edition of the Complete Psychological Works of Sigmund Freud*, Volume XIV. London: The Hogarth Press and the Institute of Psychoanalysis, pp. 237–258.

Freud, S. (1918). From the history of an infantile neurosis. In *The Standard Edition of the Complete Psychological Works of Sigmund Freud*, Volume XVII. London: The Hogarth Press and the Institute of Psychoanalysis, pp. 1–124.

Freud, S. (1920). Beyond the pleasure principle. In *The Standard Edition of the Complete Psychological Works of Sigmund Freud*, Volume XVIII. London: The Hogarth Press and the Institute of Psychoanalysis, pp. 1–64.

Freud, S. (1923). The ego and the id. In *The Standard Edition of the Complete Psychological Works of Sigmund Freud*, Volume XIX London: The Hogarth Press and the Institute of Psychoanalysis, pp. 1–66.

Freud, S. (1924). The economic problem of masochism. In *The Standard Edition of the Complete Psychological Works of Sigmund Freud*, Volume XIX London: The Hogarth Press and the Institute of Psychoanalysis, pp. 155–170.

Freud, S. (1926). Inhibitions, symptoms and anxiety. In *The Standard Edition of the Complete Psychological Works of Sigmund Freud*, Volume XX London: The Hogarth Press and the Institute of Psychoanalysis, pp. 75–176.

Freud, S. (1937). Analysis terminable and interminable. In *The Standard Edition of the Complete Psychological Works of Sigmund Freud*, Volume XXIII London: The Hogarth Press and the Institute of Psychoanalysis, pp. 209–254.

Freud, S. (1940). An outline of psycho-analysis. In *The Standard Edition of the Complete Psychological Works of Sigmund Freud*, Volume XXIII London: The Hogarth Press and the Institute of Psychoanalysis, pp. 139–208.

Gaddini, E. (1972). Aggression and the pleasure principle: Towards a psychoanalytic theory of aggression. In *A Psychoanalytic Theory of Infantile Experience*. Limentani, A. (editor). London and New York: Tavistock/Routledge, 1992, pp. 35–45.

Gaddini, E. (1982). Early defensive fantasies and the psychoanalytical process. *Int. J. Psychoanal.*, 63: 379–388.

Gaddini, R. (2002). The mother's nipple and primary identification. Personal communication, Rome, 2 July.

Gaddini, R. (2003). The precursors of transitional objects and phenomena. *Psychoanalysis and History*, 5: 53–61. Reference to *The Journal of the Squiggle Foundation*, 1: 49–57, 1985.

Green, A. (1986). The dead mother. In *On Private Madness*. London: The Hogarth Press and the Institute of Psychoanalysis, pp. 142–173. Reference to *Narcissisme vie: Narcissisme de mort*. Paris: Minuit, 1983.

Jones, E. (1955). *Sigmund Freud: Life and Work*, Volume 2. London: The Hogarth Press.

Jones, E. (1957). *Sigmund Freud, Life and Work*, Volume 3: The Last Phase 1919–1939. London: The Hogarth Press.

Joseph, B. (1982). Addiction to near-death. *Int. J. Psychoanal.*, 63: 449–456.

Loewald, H. W. (1962). The superego and the ego-ideal. *Int. J. Psychoanal.*, 43: 264–268.

Ricoeur, P. (2009). *Living Up to Death*. Chicago: The University of Chicago Press.

Salonen, S. (2004). The conceptual space of psychoanalysis. In *Power of Understanding: Essays in Honour of Veikko Tähkä*. Laine, A. (editor). London: H. Karnac Books, pp. 251–259.

Sandler, J. and Nagera, H. (1963). Aspects of the metapsychology of fantasy. *Psychoanal. Study Child*, 18: 159–194.

Schur, M. (1972). *Freud: Living and Dying*. New York: Int. Univ. Press.

Stern, M. M. (1988). Repetition and trauma. In *Toward a Teleonomic Theory of Psychoanalysis*. Hillsdale, Hove and London: The Analytic Press.

Stoloff, J.-C. (2013). On the paternal function. A paper read at the 8th Delphi International Psychoanalytic Symposium 21–24 June – Delphi, Greece.

Tähkä, V. (1993). *The Mind and Its Treatment*. Madison, CT, London: International Univ. Press, Inc.

13

RECONCILIATION WITH THE PAST

In this concluding chapter, I will examine radical psychic trauma and attempt to answer the question of how it is possible for an individual to sustain his or her psychic integrity and interest in life, regardless of the misfortunes confronted, taking unconscious psychic reality as my starting point. This realm poses a lifelong challenge not only for a psychoanalyst but for every human being. In less fortunate instances, it forms a dreadful battlefield from which many return injured and some never return at all. In his posthumous notes *Findings, Ideas and Problems* (1938) Freud touched upon this problem, writing that just as the species may perish by failing to adapt to the external world so may the individual perish from his or her internal conflicts.

For my generation of psychoanalysts, born around World War II, the Nazi genocide of the Jews, the Shoah, became a paradigm for understanding radical psychic trauma and the problem of survival. This catastrophe vastly surpassed the survivors' capacity for psychic representation; this was also true for those who received horrifying eyewitness accounts. The working through of this collective psychic trauma is still an ongoing process in Western culture.

The Shoah coerced the Jewish people into embodying the apocalyptic primal scene of their persecutors, acted out in a delusional setting of death and dying, orchestrated by a delusional mastermind. The concentration camps embodied the murderous grandeur of men who wished to eliminate people who reminded them of their humiliation, shame, and guilt – human intra-psychic conflict – and consequently individual autonomy. Therefore, the Jews were enslaved and exterminated. For the victims, this delusion signified a nightmare indistinguishable from the prevailing external reality, making it extremely difficult for them to awake and face their incredible loss and begin the work of mourning, which became a burden for many subsequent generations. Concerning the perpetrators, their collapsed ego-ideal was replaced by a delusional ideology incapable of forming a frame of reference for the psychic representation of destructive drive phenomena on the individual level, resulting not only in the acting out of destruction but also an incapacity to feel guilt, remorse and sorrow, the result of which signified the loss of their personal integrity and human dignity (Lifton, 1986; Salonen, 1997; Chasseguet-Smirgel, 2004).

Psychic reality from temporal perspective

Freud's wise recommendation that a psychoanalytic case history should be written only after the termination of the analysis underlines the importance of the temporal perspective for understanding unconscious psychic processes. This also applies to the appraisal of the analyst's work and the development of his or her conceptual thinking. Amid the daily struggle with burdensome and perplexing transferences and counter-transferences, the analyst may not be sufficiently free to perceive larger perspectives unless retroactively – *nachträglich* – to use Freud's famous notion. That is not possible without first acquiring in-depth clinical experience, with its victories and defeats. If genuinely internalised, this experience forms an interface for the analyst to approach unconscious psychic reality.

Psychoanalytic work is embedded, both in the analysand as well as in the analyst's actual life, as reflected in the analytic setting, forming an endless source of new metaphors with which to approach those unconscious psychic processes seeking articulation in the transference. The issue is not only one of living language, but also the social and cultural context at large, including psychoanalytic method and theory as a legacy from previous generations of analysts. Participation in this heritage is not only an intellectual challenge but also revitalises the analytic setting.

Although psychoanalytic experience becomes deeply imprinted on the preconscious ego of both participants, the analyst and the analysand, it does not, however, leave much external evidence capable of being discussed outside the analytic situation. Therefore, psychoanalytic case histories are needed. It is easy to agree with Paul Ricoeur (1977) that individual case histories constitute the primary texts of psychoanalytic inquiry. They form eyewitness accounts of unconscious dramas shared and lived through in the transference and counter-transference as an expression of the analysand's unconscious psychic reality. In fact, case histories constitute a crucial part of the psychoanalytic archives, containing evidence of a realm of human reality which usually evades conscious reflection.

Ricoeur's book *Memory, History, Forgetting* (2004) deals with the problems of history-writing also in the light of Freud's metapsychological thinking. From Ricoeur's perspective, Freud's theory culminates in his two works, *Remembering, Repeating and Working-Through* (1914a) and *Mourning and Melancholia* (1917). Ricoeur's starting point was that a cherished object belonging definitively to the past can be integrated as a living memory through the process of painful mourning. Conversely, an obliterated memory forms a danger to the individual's sense of reality. For Ricoeur, history-writing is an analogical process of working through on the public level, which aims to reconstruct a shared memory of the past in order to be able to live in the present and embrace the future. According to Ricoeur, history-writing is something akin to a sepulchre: a public place for mourning.

Ricoeur's notion of historiography as a remedy can be applied to psychoanalysis both as an individual process and a scientific and cultural tradition, building on the work of previous generations of analysts. Writing a case history includes an element of the work of mourning, particularly in those cases where the analytic process has been traumatically interrupted without an opportunity for working through the loss in the transference. Each case history also epitomises working through the contribution of previous generations of analysts by attempting to reconstruct not only ideationally, but also affectively in one's mind, how previous generations were working and thinking. An additional question concerning psychoanalytic writing concerns what kind of legacy we are going to leave behind – a living or a petrified one?

In Ricoeur's work, the Shoah forms a paradigmatic event for history-writing. How can we approach a catastrophe which vastly transcends the limits of an individual's comprehension? And how can we do justice to the immense loss and suffering ensuing from this catastrophe? Referring to Saint Augustine, Ricoeur reflected that the Shoah signified a *massa perdita*, an abysmal loss of human life, leading us to consider the problem of Evil. When Ricoeur (2009) returned to this problem in his posthumous fragments of essays entitled *Living Up to Death*, he emphasised the evidentiary value of testimony given by writers like Primo Levi and Jorge Semprun, both of whom were concentration camp survivors (Titelman, 2006).

In his *Literature or Life (1998)*, Jorge Semprun described an oppressive nightmare haunting him after his liberation from Buchenwald. This was related not only to the concentration camp itself but perhaps more compellingly to the traumatic collapse of his psychic boundaries, resulting in an intrapsychic fusion with the *massa perdita*. As a result, the author no longer felt alive but instead experienced himself as a ghost from the Realm of Death. A decisive step toward his recovery was an incidental meeting with a lively young woman, and watching with her a movie which unexpectedly included a scene from Buchenwald. The author had not told his friend that he was a former inmate. Only upon watching the movie was he able to conceive of the camp as a part of external reality, separate from his haunting nightmare, and since this incident, he was able to forget it at times and return to his ordinary life, differentiated from his intrapsychic fusion with death and dying. However, more than four decades were necessary before Jorge Semprun was able to revisit Buchenwald and share his memories with the younger generation. This not only evoked painful memories of the atrocities but also of the fraternity and care he experienced with other inmates. This meant, that is, an integrated memory of the traumatic past, indicating the author's psychic survival.

Jorge Semprun's autobiography illustrates the same enigmatic phenomenon that I have observed in treating severely traumatised patients in the analytic setting, namely, the recovery of their normal psychic functioning in the presence of another human being which restored their sense of reality and inner vitality. Jorge Semprun's nightmare was replaced by an inner frame of reference for the psychic representation of destructive drive phenomena. Hence it was possible to situate the immense catastrophe within a defined space and time. Buchenwald itself was transformed into a memorial of an unmitigated loss and a reminder of the individual's fundamental ambivalence in facing death and dying, which also implies the painful understanding that analogical atrocities will also be possible in the future.

After locating the Shoah in time and space, we can perhaps understand that the integration of radical psychic trauma into the temporal continuity of an individual life is an essential issue for psychoanalysis. Only that which has been acknowledged as a part of one's past is it possible to locate as an integrated whole within the dimensions of psychoanalytic metapsychology, the living memory of a lost primary object being the final organiser of the human mind. In the analytic setting, the issue is not only linked to the silent disasters in the analysand's past, compulsively repeated in the transference, or the traumatic ruptures in the analyst's life. The same also applies to the painful ruptures in the history of the psychoanalytic community, which have impeded creative thinking.

Over one hundred years of psychoanalytic experience has taught us much about the limitations of our method and has helped us understand that it is a vulnerable frame of reference for the psychic representation of elementary drive phenomena. This frame, limited in space and time, configures the psychoanalytic setting, and simultaneously defines the field of the analyst's concern. The analyst's primary task is to ensure the integrity of this constellation, which is often threatened by the intrusion of destructive drive phenomena, leading not only to a stagnation of the analytic process but also to a corruption of the analyst's thinking.

In referring to this danger, Jacqueline Amati Mehler (2004) maintained that the psychoanalytic setting is the most enduring part of Freud's creation. She argues that theory has been in a process of change since Freud's time, but not the setting. Amati Mehler is not referring to the external signs of the psychoanalytic method, but its essence: the inner constellation that frames the analytic process evolving within the dimensions of the developing theory. She believes the compromises made in the setting, often based on a misconception of psychoanalytic neutrality, easily result in a syncretistic fragmentation of theoretical thinking. As genuinely internalized, the psychoanalytic setting represents a living frame of reference for the psychic representation of disruptive drive phenomena. Instead of repeating themselves compulsively in the analysand's life, these psychic elements may find a metaphorical representation in the analytic setting, and become integrated in terms of drive-instinctual dangers as a living part of the analysand's life.

Peter Hartocollis (1976) approached the question of time from two different points of view. First, he dealt with it as an individual experience of duration, depending on the drive-instinctual expectations at the moment and following the pleasure principle. Second, Hartocollis analysed time as a *perspective in life*: that is, an affect state that transcends this basic modality of psychic regulation.

I was confronted with this problem in studying the sense of reality from the viewpoint of the individual body (Chapter 10). In this study, the body was seen as a primary narcissistic investment of vital functions, forming the foundation for the experience of being alive. But not only that; the body also conveys a preconscious understanding that one's time is limited. Thus, the temporal perspective in life depends not only on the persistence of vital drive instinctual cathexes beyond primal repression, but also on the capacity for mourning. In short, we have reached that realm of psychic reality that Freud dealt with in terms of the life instinct and the death instinct, that realm that still forms a major challenge to psychoanalytic thinking.

On the foundations of psychic survival

What originally struck me about my psychotic patients was an enigmatic fragmentation of their person, which evoked in me an impression of lifeless diffusion, difficult to explain until I encountered Freud's notion of *primal repression* (1915) I assumed that the theoretical solution to the problem of schizophrenic fragmentation lies concealed beyond primal repression, in a realm which never becomes conscious as such. However, it becomes perceptible in a schizophrenic disorder as a loss of inner vitality and diffuse fragmentation of the entire representational world. From this observation, I inferred a psychic matrix on the frontier between somatic and psychic processes. I designated it as the *primal representative matrix*, carrying inner vitality and the experience of being alive. A schizophrenic disorder manifests a drive-energetic decathexis of this matrix, with far-reaching consequences.

Another approach to the vital foundations of psychic experience was to analyse pathological affect states. André Green (1977) maintained that affects are registered before the mental apparatus is capable of forming memory traces of ideational perceptions. Therefore, supplying the ideational content to what was primally experienced as unbound excitation is a fundamental task of the psychic apparatus. If this process fails, we are confronted with pathological affect infiltrations typical of psychic trauma. With special reference to the primal representative matrix, it is possible to conceive of it as consisting of the infant's first affect responses to maternal intimacy, conveying the sense of being alive. The dissociation of this vital link leads to a collapse of affect experience, which received a trenchant description in Freud's *Mourning and Melancholia* (1917).

In normal psychic functioning, the body and its vital functions provide the most immediate contact with reality which we perceive as life, and which receives preconscious meanings in relation to other human beings. The primal representative matrix can be seen as the carrier of these meanings. The delight of being alive belongs to them. Conversely, the collapse of this matrix signifies an agonising loss. Analogous to the victims of the Shoah, many psychotic individuals have experienced this loss, which is too painful to recover from and re-establish lost confidence in life. What is then at stake is the choice between life and death, not only in a metaphorical sense. The major problem to which Freud sought a solution in his later drive theory was how to integrate this ambivalence within the totality of an individual's life (Jones, 1957).

Furthermore, we can approach extreme psychic trauma by analysing our affect responses to a newborn. Spontaneously, we feel affection and delight in seeing a delicate human being who, representing following generations, is likely to survive us. It is not only our narcissism projected onto the infant (Freud, 1914b), but it also evokes a re-vitalisation of our primary narcissism as a resource of individual well-being, carrying an anticipation of the future in the capacity of the ego-ideal.

Conversely, the helpless infant may also provoke an all-pervasive rage and envy which threaten our coherence, and in the most unfortunate cases may result in violent deeds bypassing psychic representation (Campbell and Enckell, 2005). These responses to a newcomer indicate an individual's fundamental ambivalence in facing the vulnerability of one's primary narcissistic attachment to life.

In *Death Drive, Ambivalence, and Narcissism* (1971) Kurt Eissler asked why human aggression dramatically exceeds what is necessary for self-preservation. He comes to the conclusion that aggression, narcissism, and individual ambivalence form a lethal combination. My answer to his question would be that the vulnerability of an individual's primary narcissistic attachment to life may lead the deserted ego to respond with devastating aggression in being confronted with the depletion of its primary narcissistic resources. This response forms an ultimate defence against despair. The pivotal question remaining is how it is possible to deal with this fundamental ambivalence in the psychoanalytic setting. Generally speaking, the issue is dealing with elementary drive phenomena in the transference, binding them in terms of drive-instinctual dangers to the intrapsychic conflict on the structural level of psychic functioning. The solution to this conflict also signifies the integration of vital ambivalence, which forms a counterpoint to the individual succumbing to despair.

Primary identification

The German prefix *ur-*, translated into English as 'primal', was used by Freud to refer to primeval ages of prehistory leaving certain memory traces in the human psychic constitution. In his post-Lamarckian reflections on the origins of the Oedipus complex, Freud linked his pivotal observations in the analytic setting with certain drive-instinctual deeds accomplished in the distant past, seeking expression in the transference as phantasies of incest, castration, and parricide: i.e., *primal phantasies*. Although imaginary in nature, they are perceived as actual deeds before receiving psychic representation at a preconscious level of psychic functioning. To reach this level, a crucial metaphorical transformation is needed in the rudimentary ego, that is, primary identification.

Identification was the main theme of the 34th International Psychoanalytic Congress in Hamburg in 1985. It was the first time the Congress was organised in Germany after the Holocaust, which was reflected in the Congress programme (Chasseguet-Smirgel, 2004). When primary identification was discussed, the majority of participants regarded it as an aspect of the infant's early fusion with its mother, without bestowing upon this concept a specific position in psychoanalytic vocabulary. Eugenio Gaddini belonged to those who represented the opposing view. In this connection, we had an opportunity to discuss this question only two months before his unexpected death. Through his observations of infantile experience, and my clinical experience with schizophrenic patients, we had no difficulties in agreeing that primary identification denotes a pivotal change in the conditions of the primordial ego. This meeting was very important in the development of my theoretical thinking.

With somatosensory perceptions as his starting point, Gaddini (1992) came to a profound understanding of the earliest identification phenomena. He observed that in the wake of severe maternal deprivation, the infant learns to imitate certain sensations initially related to the mother's presence by inducing physiological changes within its body, reminiscent of maternal intimacy. According to Gaddini, these 'fantasies in the body' serve not only as a defence against regression to the stage of primary unintegration (Winnicott, 1975, pp. 149–154), but also contribute to the organisation of the primordial self. In fact, Gaddini linked the urge for survival to this configuration, designating it as basic mental organisation. The same psychosensory configuration manifests itself later in the image of a circle relating to annihilation anxiety. From the theoretical point of view, it is important to note that this elementary psychic formation is not primarily derived from the oral-incorporative wishes for having an object, but from an earlier urge to be the object, according to Freud (1938) in his posthumous note on primary identification. Primary identification creates the foundation for the sense of being.

It is important to understand that the psychosensory formation described by Gaddini is a metaphor. It creates a preliminary frame of reference not only for self-object differentiation but also the psychic representation of elementary drive phenomena. Within this configuration, instinctual drives receive their first preconscious meanings in relation to the object world, accordingly to their libidinal or aggressive nature. The pleasure principle becomes anchored to the same metaphorical configuration. I owe a debt to André Green (1986, p. 166) for helping me to understand the connection between primary identification and psychic representation. According to Green, the fading of the early object of fusion leaves behind a framing-structure for a primordial matrix for the future cathexes to evolve in analogy with my notion of primal representative matrix. This point has helped me understand the fundamental importance of primary identification for the capacity of psychic representation and metaphorical thinking.

The theme of primary identification has been discussed throughout this book from different perspectives, often related to radical psychic trauma, signifying a collapse of the capacity for psychic representation. When they occur in the analytic setting, these situations may prove traumatic for the analyst as well. However, it is just these states of perplexity and confusion that may contribute to a renewal of the analyst's conceptual thinking. Like the disappearance of the primary object, it is also possible to rediscover the lost analytic insight at a new level of theoretical understanding. Hence, the psychoanalytic knowledge may be extended to an area where nothing was known to exist earlier. I think psychoanalysis, in general, develops through such a dialogue proceeding like an ascending spiral in the dimension of time, a viewpoint that Paola Marion (2012) associated with Freud's notion of *Nachträglichkeit*. This development is analogical to the child's primal scene concealing the enigma of the parents' love life, which can only be understood retroactively in the course of individual life.

From the primal scene to the genital level of psychic organisation

The notion of the primal scene, in German *Urzsene*, refers to a stage or vision of sexual intercourse conceived by the child as a horrifying, often anal-sadistic constellation. Although related to some perceptions of the parents' love life, the crucial point is not the perception itself but the fact that the child becomes confronted with the emerging drive in himself (Green, 1986). As a result of being still unable to bind his or her sexual excitations, the child experiences this as a horrifying creature comprised of a parental couple, exemplified by the Theban Sphinx in the Oedipus myth.

Children's night terror attacks, which Max Stern (1988) regarded as a paradigm of psychic trauma, help us to approach the atmosphere of the primal scene. Typical of these attacks is a feeling of desolate stimulation often related to some distressing sound. An experience of being lost in a familiar environment also belongs to this nightmare. After having temporarily lost the capacity for psychic representation, the child cannot find words to characterise this state. What is also remarkable is that often by hearing the mother's voice calling or feeling her touch the child's sense of reality is restored, including spatiotemporal apprehension signifying the recovery of primary identification.

In his *The Ego and the Id* (1923) Freud related primary identification to object-finding preceding ordinary object ties, and contributing to the emergence of the ego-ideal. He attributed primary identification to the early father, although he also considered the possibility that both parents might be involved. I grasped Freud's point more clearly as a result of writing the case history of Martin, who was a fatherless son (Salonen, 2011). In his long analysis, Martin was able to remove the unconscious obstacles not only to meeting his father for the first time in reality but also to recognising in him, instead of a monstrous figure from the primal scene, a human being capable of acknowledging Martin as his son. This critical moment signified for Martin the recovery of primary identification and the discovery of his paternity on a genital level of psychic organisation. In Martin's case, finding the father meant the confirmation of the son's right to a separate psychic existence, instead of drowning in an abysmal intrapsychic fusion with his mother. He no longer felt himself to be a nameless nonentity full of murderous hatred, but instead a person capable of feeling genuine sorrow.

Primary identification precedes the triangulation of the infant's inner world, inaugurating the Oedipus complex (Loch and Jappe, 1974; Amati Mehler, 2004, 2013; Eickhoff, 2011). The presence of the father in the child's mind frames a vital primary narcissistic resource at the ego's disposal. Within this constellation, object libidinal and aggressive urges will become bound into drive-instinctual wishes capable of seeking satisfaction in the object world. Thus, the primal representative matrix plays a uniting and vitalising role, perhaps analogous to what Freud granted *Eros*, combining things together and vitalising experience. Conversely, the decathexis of this matrix signifies a depletion of primary narcissistic resources at the ego's disposal, signifying psychic death (Winnicott, 1974). Projected onto the future, the early configuration of primary identification defines the ego ideal. At the advanced level of psychic organisation, the ego–ideal represents a counterpoint to an unbound narcissistic excitation and rude superego demands rooted not only in the castrating Oedipal father but also the child's agonies at the pre-oedipal level.

To delve into our topic further, we have to return to the infant's bodily intimacy with the mother. In visiting the archaeological exhibition *Incas and Their Predecessors: Three Millennia of Pre-Columbian Peru* at the Tampere Art Museum (2001), I was introduced to the Incas' belief that as long as women are weaving, the world will continue to exist. One can hardly find a more appropriate metaphor for the mother's importance to her child's psychic survival (Enckell, 2002, 2005). Does not the primal representative matrix become originally interwoven within the sensorial bodily intimacy with the mother, thus receiving its vital meanings? In view of Winnicott's notion of *primary maternal preoccupation* (1975, pp. 300–305) and Bion's concept of the *mother's reverie* (1962), we can understand that through this kind of dialogue with its mother, the infant discovers a vital drive-instinctual resource in himself (R. Gaddini, 1981).

From the object-libidinal point of view, the mother's subtle psychic work decisively contributes to the infant's interest in life in the sense of having an object, primarily the mother's breast. In addition, the mother also contributes to the infant becoming capable of surviving bereavement and loss at different levels of psychic development. Besides delight in motherhood, primary maternal preoccupation also includes an aspect of sorrow: the mother's silent work of mourning, containing her psychic pain. The mother's capacity to mourn reflects her psychic integrity attained by resolving her vital ambivalence and her intrapsychic conflict at the genital level of psychic organisation, signifying that her own narcissistic and object-libidinal interests are in balance.

Thus, in weaving together both the psychosensory and object-libidinal aspects of infantile experience, the mother decisively contributes to the infant's psychic survival, although her contribution may only become perceptible retroactively, namely in her child's capacity not only to love but also survive loss in the course of life without succumbing to despair. The capacity to survive derived from maternal intimacy is tragically absent in those cases where primary maternal preoccupation has failed. Ms O's case history epitomises all of the inner destruction unleashed by this failure. Conversely, when the mother's psychic work is successfully internalised, it carries her children's future as a constituent of their ego ideal. I refer to the memory of the lost primary object as the final organiser of an individual's mind.

Which process combines the maternal and paternal constituents of primary identification? I would like to propose that it is the parents' genital love life that frames the metaphorical space into which the child is born, represented by the 'other room' in the analytic setting, referring to Ronald Britton's work on the significance of parental sexuality in the Oedipus complex (Britton, 1989, 1998). The infant's father in the mother's mind already evokes this metaphorical space, extending into the future and conveying the belief that the father can be rediscovered in the real world outside the maternal fusion-object. Finding the real father then confirms this expectation, consolidating the child's ego-ideal in the frame of which the Oedipus complex will be dealt with and finally resolved at the genital level of psychic organisation. In this sense, the child's father in the mother's mind represents hope for the child, corresponding to Donald Winnicott's view at the end of his life (Abram, 2013)

The crux of my study centres on genital love as an organising principle for the evolving human mind, represented by the parents for their child. The profound preconscious significance of the parents' love life will be understood only retroactively, in the course of an individual's life, perhaps after working through the nightmares of the primal scene in the psychoanalytic setting. May not this developmental achievement conceal a subtle delight that Paul Ricoeur called a 'happy' memory in his great work on history-writing:

> And why should we not refer in fine to Beethoven's last quartets and sonatas and to their powerful evocation of sublime sadness?

There, the word has been uttered: sublimation. This missing piece in the panoply of Freud's metapsychology might perhaps have provided him with the secret of the reversal from the complaisance toward sadness to sadness sublimated – into joy. Yes, grief is that sadness that has not completed the work of mourning. Yes, joy is the reward of giving up the lost object and a token of the reconciliation with its internalized object. And, inasmuch as the work of mourning is the required path for the work of remembering *souvenir*, joy can also crown with its grace the work of memory (*mémoire*). On the horizon of this work: a "happy" memory, when the poetic image completes the work of mourning. But this horizon recedes behind the work of history, the theory of which has yet to be established beyond the phenomenology of memory.

(Ricoeur, 2004, p. 77)

Ricoeur's text brings to mind Freud's (1917) profound interpretation of melancholia, which he related to an injured primary narcissism signifying agonising pain and the paralysis of the ego. The advanced ego-ideal forms the structural counterpoint to this calamity, signifying not only a happy memory of the lost primary object but also the sublimation of untamed primary narcissism, experienced as the delight of being alive. Through the work of mourning, the ego may recover its primary narcissistic resources at the advanced level of psychic functioning, which also signifies a progressive internalisation of the past and anticipation of the future. To the extent that this transformation has taken place, a wounded primary narcissism becomes possible to accept as a sad occurrence in the individual's history or prehistory, belonging to the past without there being endless demands for retribution. This state of mind is not removed from the delight of being alive, the clarity of vision, and the capability for transparent thinking, all of which indicates an individual psychic survival.

References

Abram, J. (2013). DWD's notes for the Vienna Congress 1971: A consideration of Winnicott's theory of aggression and an interpretation of the clinical implications. In *Donald Winnicott Today*. Abram, J. (editor). Chapter 14. New Library of Psychoanalysis and the Institute of Psychoanalysis. London: Routledge.

Amati Mehler, J. (2004). Der psycho-sensorische Bereich in Neurose und Psychose. *Jahrb. Psychoanal.*, 49: 113–135.

Amati Mehler, J. (2013). The vicissitudes of fatherhood. A paper read at the *8th Delphi International Psychoanalytic Symposium*, 21–24 June – Delphi, Greece.

Bion, W. R. (1962). *Learning from Experience*. London: Tavistock.

Britton, R. (1989). The missing link: Parental sexuality in the Oedipus complex. In *The Oedipus Complex Today Clinical Implications*. Chapter 2. Britton, R., Feldman, M. and O'Shaugnessy, E. (editors). London: H. Karnac, pp. 83–101.

Britton, R. (1998). *Belief and Imagination: Explorations in Psychoanalysis*. The New Library of Psychoanalysis. London: Routledge.

Campbell, D. and Enckell, H. (2005). Metaphor and violent act. *Int. J. Psychoanal.*, 86: 801–882.

Chasseguet-Smirgel, J. (2004). Trauma und Glauben. *Jahrb. Psychoanal.*, 49: 39–53.

Eickhoff, F.-W. (2011). Ein Plädoyer für das umstrittene Konzept der primären Identifizierung. *Psyche – Z. Psychoanal.*, 65: 63–83.

Eissler, K. (1971). Death drive, ambivalence, and narcissism. *Psychoanal. Study Child*, 26: 25–78.

Enckell, H. (2002). *Metaphor and the Psychodynamic Function of the Mind*. Kuopio: Kuopio University Publications D. Medical Sciences 265.

Enckell, H. (2005). On the metapsychology of affects. *Scand. Psychoanal. Rev.*, 28: 22–30.

Freud, S. (1914a). Remembering, repeating and working-through. (Further recommendations on the technique of psycho-analysis II). In *The Standard Edition of the Complete Psychological Works of Sigmund Freud*, Volume XII, pp. 145–156.

Freud, S. (1914b). On narcissism. In *The Standard Edition of the Complete Psychological Works of Sigmund Freud*, Volume XIV, pp. 67–102.

Freud, S. (1915). Repression. In *The Standard Edition of the Complete Psychological Works of Sigmund Freud*, Volume XIV, pp. 141–158.

Freud, S. (1917). Mourning and melancholia. In *The Standard Edition of the Complete Psychological Works of Sigmund Freud*, Volume XIV, pp. 237–258.

Freud, S. (1923). The ego and the id. In *The Standard Edition of the Complete Psychological Works of Sigmund Freud*, Volume XIX, pp. 1–66.

Freud, S. (1938). Findings, ideas, problems. In *The Standard Edition of the Complete Psychological Works of Sigmund Freud*, Volume XXIII, pp. 299–300.

Gaddini, E. (1992). *A Psychoanalytic Theory of Infantile Experience*. Limentani, A. (editor). London: Tavistock and Routledge.

Gaddini, R. (1981). Bion's "Catastrophic Change" and Winnicott's "Breakdown". *Rivista Di Psicoanalisi*, 27: 610–621.

Green, A. (1977). Conceptions of affect. *Int. J. Psychoanal.*, 58: 129–156.

Green, A. (1986). The dead mother. In *On Private Madness*. London: The Hogarth Press and the Institute of Psychoanalysis, pp. 142–173. Reference to *Narcissisme vie: Narcissisme de mort*. Paris: Minuit, 1983.

Hartocollis, P. (1976). On the experience of time and its dynamics, with special reference to affects. *J. Amer. Psychoanal. Assn.*, 24: 363–375.

Jones, E. (1957). *Sigmund Freud: Life and Work*, Volume Three: The Last Phase 1919–1939. London: The Hogarth Press, pp. 493–494.

Lifton, R. J. (1986). *The Nazi Doctors: Medical Killing and the Psychology of Genocide*. London: Macmillan.

Loch, W. and Jappe, G. (1974). Die Konstruktion der Wirklichkeit und die Phantasien: Anmerkungen zu Freuds Krankengeschichte des "Kleinen Hans". *Psyche – Z. Psychoanal.*, 28: 1–31.

Marion, P. (2012). Some reflections on the unique time of Nachträglichkeit in theory and clinical practice. *Int. J. Psychoanal.*, 93: 317–340.

Ricoeur, P. (1977). The question of proof in Freud's psychoanalytic writings. *J. Amer. Psychoanal. Assn.*, 25: 835–871.

Ricoeur, P. (2004). *Memory, History, Forgetting*. Chicago: The University of Chicago Press.

Ricoeur, P. (2009). *Living Up to Death*. Chicago: The University of Chicago Press.

Salonen, S. (1997). Humiliation and dignity: Reflections on ego integrity. In *Seed of Madness: Constitution, Environment, and Fantasy in the organization of The Psychotic Core*. Volkan, V. D. and Akhtar, S. (editors). Madison, CT: Int. Univ. Press, pp. 59–79.

Salonen, S. (2011). The absent father in the transference: A case study of primary identification and psychic survival. *Scand. Psychoanal. Rev.*, 34: 85–94.

Semprun, J. (1998). *Literature or Life*. New York: Penguin Books.

Stern, M. M. (1988). *Repetition and Trauma: Toward a Teleonomic Theory of Psychoanalysis*. Hillsdale, Hove and London: The Analytic Press.

Tampere Art Museum (2001). Incas and their predecessors – three millennia of pre-Columbian Peru. In *Exhibition Catalogue*. Korpisaari, A., Pennanen, T. and Ilmonen, A. (editors). Tampere: Tampereen taidemuseon julkaisuja, p. 95.

Titelman, D. (2006). Primo Levi's loneliness: Psychoanalytic perspectives on suicide-nearness. *Psychoanal. Q.*, 75: 835–858.

Winnicott, D. W. (1974). Fear of breakdown. *Int. Rev. Psychoanal.*, 1: 103–107.

Winnicott, D. W. (1975). *Through Paediatrics to Psychoanalysis*. London: The Hogarth Press and the Institute of Psychoanalysis.

Index

Abram, Jan 6
affect 6, 8; affective validation 71; bodily dimension of 63–65; drive dimension of 65–66; integration 62–63, 68; recovery of 62–73; vital affects 82, 99, 108
affectomotor 50, 64
aggression 3, 5, 18, 41, 91–105; vicarious release of 63
Alanen, Yrjö 12
Amati Mehler, Jacqueline 148, 157
ambivalence 4, 32, 72, 101; integration of 138–141; related to children 111; toward death and dying 108
anal-destructive 28–29
anger 67–68
Anlehnung 110
annihilation 53–59, 64: anxiety 28, 40–41; threat of 3, 78
anxiety 78, 83, 102; *see also* annihilation
apathy 37, 68
Augustine, Saint 155
Autism 40
autonomy 88, 104

β-elements 51, 142
Baranger *et al.* 52
basic mental organisation 114
Bion, Wilfred 6–8, 39, 51, 114, 142, 163
birth 5, 27, 57; animal 142; denial of 96; still birth 30, 42
Blum, Harold 41
body 29, 38, 67–68; and affect 63–65; and sense of reality 108–117; vital bodily functions 110; *see also* castration; erogeneity; genital reality; mind-body continuum
breast 7, 28, 43–44, 56, 83, 102, 103, 109, 115, 126–129, 163
Britton, Ronald 164

castration 22, 38, 51, 88, 98; castration anxiety 22, 25–33, 45, 68, 72
catastrophic change 49
cathexis 20, 39
Chasseguet-Smirgel, Janine 27, 28–29, 123, 148
consolidation 13, 71

Index

container 42, 45, 52, 70, 114, 146–147, 150; *container/contained* 39
cosmic mode of experience 36, 40, 43
creativity 98

death 3, 37, 41, 48–49, 69, 86–87, 112–113; anality and 29; in dualistic drive theory 98; instinct 85, 92–93; *see also* drives: death drive; suicide
decathexis 16–17, 21, 50, 103–104, 114
defence: and early somatic responses 64; formation of 36–37
deferred action see *Nachträglichkeit*
depression: depressive moods 30–31, 83; psychotic 63, 71–72, 112
desire see *mieliteko*
despair 72, 87, 98, 112
desperation 37
destruction 3, 62; *see also* drives: destructive drive phenomena
dialogue, inner 3, 9, 108, 114, 116, 147
differentiation 18; self-object 66, 68
disintegration 3
dissociation 29, 64, 95
dream 42–44, 65, 81–82
drives: and affects 65–66; death drive 93, 97–98, 105, 141; destructive drive phenomena 4, 41, 63, 91–105; drive conflict 8–9, 73; drive economy 9, 17–18, 20, 32, 41, 142–145; drive elements 7; drive-energetic discharge 18; drive-energetic emergency 13; drive-energetic regression 18; drive-instinctual dangers 1–2, 22, 29, 51, 88; drive-instinctual ideas 8, 51; drive-instinctual impulses 75; drive-instinctual processes 3, 22; drive-instinctual tensions 36, 99; drive-instinctual wish 49–51, 109; drive tension 50; drive theories 18; elementary drive phenomena 6, 51, 85, 88, 97; instinctual 3–4, 62, 65–66, 70, 110; life drive 98; primary drive potential 18
drug addictions 78
dualism 85
dualistic drive theory 2, 91, 93
dynamic 17

ego 45; autonomy 22; child's developing 25–33; ego-ideal 9, 51–53, 71, 85–86, 99, 114; ego-instincts 41; ego-split 17, 29; formation 39; and id-perception 51; impoverished, 21–22; metaphorical 39; primordial 35–37; and psychotic disorder 76; and radical psychic trauma 77; reality-ego 31, 32–33, 35; rudimentary 18–20, 36; vulnerable 145–147
Eissler, Kurt 94–95, 159
Eizirik, Claudio 148
Empedocles 140
Enckell, Henrik 76
erogeneity 37
Eros 92, 96, 139–140, 145, 163

Index

face 38–39, 40, 108, 127–129, 134; facial expressions 17
falling 43
fantasy 68
father 13–14, 37–38, 53–59, 68–70, 102; absent 120–134; and genital level 26–27, 31; in the primal scene 116; and primary identification 147–149, 162–164; *see also* object relations; Oedipus complex; primary identification
Federn, Paul 93
Fenichel, Otto 63–64
fetish 28–29, 31, 45, 116
fragmentation 12–15, 22, 68–69, 114–115
frame: delusional frames 78; frame of reference 76, 79; framing structure 39, 70
Freud, Anna 22, 82, 94
Freud, Sigmund 1–3, 6, 17, 18–20; on castration 26; on the death drive 140–141; on dreams 81; on drive-instinctual ideas 51; dualistic drive theory of 91–98, 105; on ego-instincts 41; on ego split 116; on erogeneity of the body 37; on fate neurosis 104; on the female sexual organ 31; on helplessness 146; on id-perception 50, 84; influences on 139–140; on melancholia 138–139, 165; metapsychological thinking of 155; *Nachträglichkeit* 137, 161; on Oedipus complex 83; on original contact with reality 35; on pain 141; on perceptual identity 84; on the pleasure principle 144–145; on primal castration 127; on primal phantasies 160; on primary identification 52–53, 76, 85–86, 113–114, 129, 142, 147, 161–162; on primary narcissism 110; on psychic functioning 109–110; on psychic trauma 39; psychic trauma of 149; on psychoanalytic case history 154; and the psychoanalytic setting 157; topographic formulations of 82; on unconscious psychic reality 153; on the unconscious wish 49
fusion 18; with destroyed primary object 72; maternal 52, 70, 85, 113

Gaddini, Eugenio: and aggression 94, 125; and basic mental organisation 55, 114; on defence development 36; on Freud 141; and primary identification 58, 70, 160–161; on psychic survival 3, 6, 147; on somatic responses in early infancy 64; on the urge for survival 40
Gaddini, Renata 143
genital reality 25–33, 51, 75–76, 116, 162–165; genital love life 28–30; of parents 25–27; and psychoanalytical setting 27; representing 44–45
Goethe, Johann Wolfgang von 51
Green, André: on affect 63, 158; on depression of the mother 1, 149; on maternal fusion 52,

70, 114, 147–148; and primary identification 6, 39, 133, 161; on temporality 3
guilt 83, 103

hallucination 36, 64–65, 67–68, 99, 129
Hartocollis, Peter 117, 157
hate 44, 62, 100–101
helplessness, traumatic 35–37, 78, 88, 98, 111
Hilflosigkeit see helplessness
Hoffer, Willi 21
holding ix, xi
hope 104
hopelessness 87
humiliation 26, 29, 72, 134, 153

id 31–33, 49; id-ideas 36; id-impulses 71; id-perception 50–51; development of 84
identification: identification phenomena 35; projective 63, 100; and psychic trauma 52–53; *see also* primary identification
identity: identity theme 76, 100–102; perceptual identity 84
Ikonen, Penti 96
imago 39
individuation 52, 88, 115, 149
influencing machine 110
integration 73, 79, 88; of affect xi; of aggression 97–98; of ambivalence xiii, 4, 9, 105, 108, 138–141; of anger 67–68; of castration anxiety 31–33; and defences 64; and depressive position 83; dialogue and 1, 3; of envy 93; first integrated image 44; first integrated thought 44; of fundamental ambivalence 4; genital level of x, 3–4; inability to attain 115; of loss 104–105; and *mother's reverie*, 7; pain of 115–116; primary unintegration 5; of vulnerability 29
internalisation 15
intimacy 99, 101
intuition 65
intrapsychic level 44; intrapsychic conflict 15, 51, 88; intrapsychic solution 8

Jacobson, Edith 12, 18, 21
Jones, Ernst 141
Joseph, Betty 141–142

Kernberg, Otto 65
Kivi, Aleksis 77
Klein, Melanie 26, 64, 70, 83, 93
Kohut, Heinz 12, 16
Krystal, Henry 111

Laplanche, Jean 25–26, 39, 70, 77
Levi, Primo 156
libido 93; libidinal dependence 95; libidinal strivings 18; libidinal wishes 88; libidinal resources 37, 105
Lichtenstein, Heinz 76
Lind, Lis 97–98
living organism: analogy of 39
Loewald, Hans 137
Loewenstein, Rudolph 99
London, Nathanael 20–21
longing 38, 51
loss 28, 30–31, 44–45; *see also* death; love; mourning

Index

love: falling in 66, 68; loss of love 22, 51, 88, 98
loyalty conflict 111

Marion, Paola 161
Martinsson, Harry 37, 43, 105
masochism 99; erotogenic 41, 56, 101
masturbation 72
McDougall, Joyce 26–27, 28, 115, 134
melancholia 112, 138–139, 165
Meltzer *et al.* 40
memory 63, 156
mental representation 44
metaphor 7–8, 27; for loss 32; metaphorical frame 6, 73; and psychic disorder 76; and transference 4, 154
metapsychology: defined, 8; Freudian 122, 165; and memory 156–157; of psychic survival 136–150; and radical psychic trauma 35; of schizophrenia 12–23
mieliteko (desire) 84
mind-body continuum 115
mortido 93; *see also* death
mother: and affects 63–65; animal 142–143; in case studies 30, 38, 42–44, 48–49, 53–59, 63, 68–70, 72, 86–87, 99–103, 120–133; and dialogue 1–2, 108–109; and genital reality 25–28; and identity 76; *mother's reverie* 163; and narcissism 95–96; in Oedipus complex 72; phallic 116, 134; and primary identification xi, 36–37, 39, 52, 160–164; primary maternal preoccupation 5, 163; and the primordial ego 36–37; and psychic survival 4–7, 147–149; in psychoanalytic thinking 83; psychosis of 14, 115; *see also* breast; object relations; primary identification; fusion
mourning 8–9, 28, 104–105, 113

Nachträglichkeit (deferred action) 137, 154, 161
narcissism 8; and destructive drive phenomena 95–96; narcissistic disorders 93; primary 18, 82, 85, 104, 110
neutralisation 18, 21
nightmare *see* dream; night terrors
night terrors 36, 162

object relations: object attachment 15; object finding 6, 52, 85, 114; object love 102; object ties 63, 66, 113; original 44; survival of 6; transitional 14–15, 40–41; and the unconscious wish 85, 88
Oedipus complex 3, 26, 70, 83; Oedipal constellation 14, 68; Oedipal desire 29; Oedipal guilt 72; Oedipal renunciation 26, 44; Oedipal solution 27, 32, 116; Oedipal surrender 26–27; Oedipal wishes 87
Ogden, Thomas 6
Oliner, Marion M. 116–117
oral-introjective area 64, 82–83

panic 37, 42–44; panic attacks 30–31
patricide 51, 72
penis 30–31, 38

phantasy 30, 38, 113; oral-cannibalistic 72, 148; oral-introjective 82; primal 65, 160
Piha, Heikki 65
pleasure 91; pleasure-ego 31, 35, 39; pleasure principle 39, 41–42, 141–142
primal representative matrix 2, 17, 41, 49, 114, 158; collapse of 22–23
primal repression 19–20, 98, 158
primal scene 26, 42–43, 51, 162–165
primary identification 2–3, 6, 53, 63–65, 70–71, 160–161; the body and 110–111, 115–116; compared to ethological imprinting 70; and the foundations of psychic experience 76–77; and psychic representation 113–115; and psychic survival 120–134; recovery of 103–104; restitution of 35–45; and the unconscious wish 85–87
psychic development 110, 114: early 18–20, 35, 52; hypothetical beginning of 50; inception of 64
psychic energy 18
psychic functioning 109–111
psychic integrity 79
psychic intensity 51
psychic reality 25; *see also* unconscious
psychic regulation 21–22, 64
psychic representation 3, 6, 12–14, 19–20, 22, 31, 51, 70, 109; of destructive drive phenomena 63; of elementary drive phenomena 97; and primary identification 113–115; representational space 39; representational world 15, 36, 70, 103
psychic survival 3, 12, 86; creativity and 98; foundations of 158–159; metapsychology of 136–150; and primary identification 120–134; unconscious foundations of 147–148
psychic trauma 41–44; and affect 63; radical 12, 35–45, 77, 153–165; reconstruction of 48–59; threat of 78
psychoanalytic thinking xi, xii, 9, 82–83, 93, 140, 158
psychosensory area 64
psychosexual development 72
psychosomatic condition 37, 78, 86–88, 111–113
psychotic conditions 75–79, 93, 104; *see also* schizophrenia

Rangell, Leo 81, 88, 97
reality: original contact with 35; reality perception 50, 71, 75; sense of 108–117
Rechardt, Eero 96
regression 38, 102–103
repetition compulsion 41–42, 86
representation *see* psychic representation
Ricoeur, Paul 144, 155–156, 164–165
Rosenblatt, B. 36
Rosenfeld, Herbert 94–96

Sandler, Anne-Marie 83
Sandler, Joseph 36, 82–83

Index

schizophrenia 12–23, 66, 109, 114; hebephrenic psychosis 12, 67; non-schizophrenic state analogical to 16–17; schizoaffective psychosis 66–70; schizo-paranoid position 83
Schmerz 93, 139
Schur, Max 31, 36, 49; on Freud 92–93, 140; on the unconscious wish 84;
secondary process level 32
self-configuration 3
self-deception 29
Semprun, Jorge 156
separation 22, 51, 88, 98
sexuality 51, 63; 'neo-sexualities' 28; origins of 25–26; sexual perversions 78
shame 28; shame-guilt dilemmas 71
Shoah, the 153–154, 155–157, 159
signal function 72; signal anxiety 21–22, 32; *see also* anxiety
skin 13, 17, 40, 102, 111, 114, 129
somatic disorders 109
somatic process 20, 22, 36, 64
sorrow 62, 70, 104
Spiegel, Leo A. 76
spiral 3, 41
Spitz, René 1, 40, 108, 114
splitting 8, 22, 31, 83, 93, 116; *see also* ego
stagnation 31, 68, 116, 157
Stein, Ruth 70, 83
Stern, Max 162
stimulation, perceptual 36–38
Stoloff, Jean-Claude 148
structure 17; elementary structures 16; psychic 14; structural conflict 62–73, 88; structuralisation 77; structural problems 15; structural theory 20, 39, 52, 70, 82
suicide 100–104
superego 51, 67, 71–72, 96, 116
survival: individual 50; urge for 40; *see also* psychic survival

Tähkä, Veikko 66, 77, 145–146
Tausk, Viktor 110–111, 114
Thanatos 96
time 150; and the body 116–117; and psychic reality 154–158
Todesangst 111
topographic theory 82, 137
transference 4, 8, 14–16, 22, 76, 79, 87, 103; and the absent father 120–134; neurosis 109; transference-countertransference 67
trauma: early 38; recovery from 41; sexual 66–70; *see also* psychic trauma
traumatic narcosis 16–17

unconscious 17, 153–165; wish 81–89
Urzsene see primal scene

vitality 38, 99, 103, 125, 156, 158; foundation for 44; and integration of castration anxiety 32; psychic 139, 148; and schizophrenia 13–22, 67
Volkan, Vamik D. 78
vulnerability 5, 78–79; individual 29; of psychic regulation 22

Index

wellbeing 36, 53, 55, 71, 110, 115, 148
Widlöcher, Daniel 85
Winnicott, Donald 4–6, 36, 163–164

wish formation 65–66; primordial wishes 49; *see also* unconscious
World War II *see* Shoah, the
Wurmser, Leon 71